My Daily Orthodox Prayer Book

Classic Orthodox Prayers for Every Need

Compiled and Edited
by
Anthony M. Coniaris

LIGHT & LIFE PUBLISHING COMPANY
Minneapolis, Minnesota

Light & Life Publishing Company
P.O. Box 26421
Minneapolis, MN 55426-0421

Copyright© 2001
Light & Life Publishing Company
Library of Congress Control. No. 2001130412

ISBN No. 1-880971-65-8

✛ *contents* ✛

sometimes God sends me moments in which I am utterly at peace. In those moments I have constructed for myself a creed in which everything is clear and holy for me. Here it is: to believe that there is nothing more beautiful, more profound, more sympathetic, more reasonable, more courageous and more perfect than Christ; and not only is there nothing but I tell myself in jealous love that never could there be. ✠

–Fyodor Dostoevsky

The Orthodox Rule of Prayer

To dedicate a period of time each day to listening to Jesus, and to prayer, is to choose, as Mary did, "the better part," "the one thing needful." It means that we have realized that meeting God in prayer is the most important thing we can do each day. We read in the Bible that God would speak to Moses "face to face" (Exodus 33:11). What a wonderful thing it is for us, too, to develop this kind of intimacy with God whereby we speak to Him in prayer each day face to face. To remind yourself that it is indeed "face to face," place an icon of Christ before you as you pray.

The people of God whose prayers are recorded in the Bible and in the prayer books of the Church, seldom ever read a book on prayer, seldom ever went to a seminar on prayer, seldom ever heard a sermon on prayer. They just prayed! And the prayers of the Church are so important because the whole theology of what we believe about God is to be found in those prayers *(lex credendi, lex orandi)*. What we believe is what we pray. And what we pray is what we believe. That is why the Church Fathers say that one who truly prays is a theologian. And a true theologian is one who prays.

Satan fears prayer because God hears prayer. Satan will stop at nothing to distract and discourage a person from prayer. If he succeeds at this, he separates us from our greatest source of power. This is why the Church Fathers keep stressing that to pray, a person must struggle to his last breath.

Power in Prayer
William Barclay has said that "in praying for those we love we must remember;
(1) the love of God that wants the best
    for them;
(2) the wisdom of God that knows
    what is best for them; and
(3) the power of God that can accomplish it."

Mother Teresa was asked once why her sisters spent several hours a day praying in chapel instead of devoting that time to their work. Mother Teresa replied, "If my sisters were not in chapel praying two or three times a day, they would not go out into the streets of Calcutta at all."

Bishop Kallistos Ware wrote,
"Remember God more often than you breathe," says St. Gregory of Nazianzus (d.389). Prayer is more essential to us, more an integral part of ourselves, than the rhythm of our breathing or the beating of our heart. Without prayer there is no life. Prayer is our nature. As human persons we are created for prayer just as we are created to speak and to think. The

*human animal is best defined, not as a logical or tool-making animal or an animal that laughs, but rather as an animal that prays, a Eucharistic animal, capable of offering the world back to God in thanksgiving and intercession."**

They Prayed...

Abraham prayed, and so long as he prayed, God did not destroy the city of Sodom   (GEN. 18:20-23).

Elijah prayed, and God sent fire from heaven to consume the offering on the altar in order to show that He is the One True God   (1 KINGS 18:17-40).

Elisha prayed, and the son of the Shunammite woman was resurrected from the dead   (2 KINGS 4:17-37).

The thief on the cross prayed and he received the answer to his prayer immediately as Jesus said to him, "Today, you will be with me in paradise"
     (LUKE 23:39-43).

Paul prayed and churches were born in Europe and Asia Minor   (ACTS 9:22-31).

Jesus prayed at the door of the tomb of Lazarus, and Lazarus who had been dead for four days, came walking out of the tomb.   (JOHN 11: 1-44).

Peter prayed and Dorcas was raised from death to life
     (ACTS 9:36-42).

---

* Praying with the Orthodox Tradition" (compiled by S. Parent). Published by Triangle SPCK. 1898. London.

No Greater Privilege

Truly, prayer is the greatest privilege we have, if only we would avail ourselves of it not just in time of trouble but every day, many times a day. I must confess personally, that I find the greatest strength to sustain me in my prayer life. If it were not for prayer, I don't know how I would be able to cope.

Talk It Over With God

So, if something is disturbing and upsetting you, talk it over with God. Pour it all out before Him, for He truly cares for you. Tell Him exactly how you feel. Remember, God is not only your Creator, your Father, but also your Friend of friends. Moses walked and talked with God as his friend. "Thus the Lord used to speak to Moses face to face, as a man speaks to his friend." As the Lord Jesus spoke with His Father, so you have not only a right but, as His child, a holy privilege to speak to Him in prayer each day face to face.

Cultivate Daily Prayer

Cultivate daily prayer with God, your Father, and accept the truth that he awaits your every call and will unfailingly respond. Isaiah says, "Call, and the Lord will answer; you shall cry, and he will say, 'Here I am'...Then shall your light rise in the darkness and your gloom be as the noonday."

Sir Isaac Newton once said,

> *I can take my telescope and look millions of miles into space; but I can go away to my room and in prayer get nearer to God and Heaven than I can when assisted by all the telescopes of earth.*

Although prayer is natural, and we were fashioned by God to live a life of prayer, sin has built a barrier between us and God. That is why prayer is hard work now. Whenever we start to pray, the devil and his legions are there to distract us and to try to steal our prayers.

What is the Rule of Prayer?

To combat this, the Orthodox Church in her great wisdom has given us what is known as the Rule of Prayer. This means that you have to set aside a regular period of time each day and devote it exclusively to prayer, to uniting yourself to God. In other words, "You cannot wait to be in the mood of prayer; you have to use the spur of your Prayer Rule to force yourself to pray," as Sergei Fudel writes in his excellent book "Light in the Darkness" (SVS PRESS).

Our Orthodox tradition also provides a basic outline of content for the Rule of Prayer which begins with a simple invocation of the name of God, i.e., we make the sign of the cross and say, "In the Name of the Father and of the Son and of the Holy Spirit. Amen." This is followed by the prayer to the Holy

Spirit, "O Heavenly King..." This is followed in turn by the Trisagion Prayers. Of course, this is only the beginning of the Rule of Prayer. It may go on and include the reading of a psalm, a Scripture reading, the Nicene Creed, some of the petitions from the liturgy, a period of silence, special petitions of praise and thanksgiving, intercessions for other people, etc. It can be as long or as short as you please. It depends on you. Remember the prayer of the thief on the Cross was very short, "Lord, remember me in your kingdom;" and the prayer of the Publican was very short, "Lord, be merciful to me, the sinner."

So, if you have not already started, begin to form a daily Rule of Prayer. Use the Trisagion prayers of the Church as the foundation upon which to build. Begin humbly and simply–but begin. You will be greatly blessed.

We pray that you will find this prayerbook to be helpful as you begin to practice your daily rule of prayer. –AMC

What is Prayer?

Prayer is the raising of the mind and heart to God in praise and thanksgiving to Him and in supplication for the good things we that we need, both spiritual and physical (St. Theophan).

- Prayer ... uplifts and unites human beings with God (St. Gregory Palamas).
- Prayer is our personal communication system with our home base.
- Prayer is a booster cable from our depleted lives to the ever dependable power of God which never fails to start us up again.
- Prayer is the response of the soul to the love of God.
- Prayer is taking our burdens to God, knowing He will help us carry them and renew us for the journey.
- Prayer is heaven in the heart...the kingdom of God within you.
- Prayer is creating an openness where God can give Himself to us.
- Prayer is Jacob's ladder by which we ascend to God and God descends to us.
- Prayer is the heart's moment to bathe itself in the beauty of God's love and the cleansing of God's care.
- Prayer is holding all people in our hearts through love (St. John of Kronstadt).

- Prayer is the descent of heaven into the soul
  (ST. JOHN OF KRONDSTADT).
- Prayer is the abiding of the most Holy Trinity in the
  soul in accordance with the words of Jesus, "We will
  come to him, and make our home in him"
  (ST. JOHN OF KRONDSTADT).
- The soul came forth from God and to God it may
  ever ascend through prayer (ST. JOHN OF KRONDSTADT).
- Prayer is remembering to call home because you are
  a child of God.
- Prayer is a matter of love. The more one loves, the
  more one prays.
- Prayer is giving my worries to God and receiving
  His peace in return (PHIL. 4:6-7). What an exchange!
- Prayer is slipping into God's presence.
- Prayer is the "hot line" between God and us–a line
  always open for communication.
- Prayer is hemming the day in with God, thus mak-
  ing it less likely to unravel.
- Prayer is what Abraham said, "May I presume to
  speak to the Lord, dust and ashes that I am?" (GEN.
  18:27). Yes! You may!
- Prayer is the empty cup standing before God asking
  to be filled.
- There are four answers to prayer: "No." Yes."
  "Wait." "I never thought you'd ask."
- Prayer is coming to God with great faith and great
  expectations:

Thou art coming to a King,
Great petitions with thee bring;
For His grace and power are such
None can ever ask too much.

• Seraphim of Thmuis wrote in a letter to his monks:
The universe is saved by your prayers; thanks to your
supplications, the rain descends on the earth, the
earth is covered in green, the trees are laden with
fruit. *

My soul is like an altar Light,
A holy fire, flickering in ruby glass
In perpetual adoration.

–Emily G. White

O my God, deep calls unto deep (Ps. 42:7)
The deep of my profound misery calls
to the deep of your infinite mercy.

–Bernard of Clairvaux

---

* (from "Introducing the Orthodox Church" by A.M. Coniaris.
Light & Life Publishing Company. Minneapolis, MN. 1982)

Praying The Daily Hours

We can learn to practice an excellent system of daily meditation from the Orthodox cycle of daily worship.

The New Testament follows a system of telling time according to which the first hour of the day is hour one after sunrise or 7:00 a.m. Hour two is 8:00 a.m. and Hour three is 9:00 a.m., etc.

Using this schedule, the early Christians would pause for prayer and meditation every third hour during the day. For example, we know that the apostles Peter and John "went up together into the temple at the hour of prayer, being the ninth hour" (ACTS 3:1). We find St. Peter praying on Simon's housetop "at the sixth hour"   (ACTS 10:9).

The monastic orders devised prayer services for common worship around the system of "hours." Their life became a constant balance between prayer and work. They would enter the sanctuary for prayer at the third hour (9:00 a.m.), the sixth hour (noon), the ninth hour (3:00 p.m.) and the twelfth (6:00 p.m.). They paused for prayer in the morning, noon, afternoon and evening. We still celebrate "the service of the hours" in every Orthodox parish every Holy Friday, Christmas and Epiphany. This New Testament way of telling time is still in use today in the monasteries of Mt. Athos.

Each of the holy cycles of prayer had a special theme which related to something in the history of salvation that happened at that hour. The worship service composed by the Church Fathers for that hour usually included scripture readings, psalms and hymns relating to that event.

We shall examine each hour with with the special purpose of helping us to pause briefly during these hours each day to meditate and pray.

The First Hour

O God, You are my God, at dawn I seek You.
                                    PS. 63:1 (SEPTUAGINT)

The first hour (hour one after the rise of the sun or 7:00 a.m.), has as its central theme the coming of the light in the dawn of a new day. The coming of the physical light reminds the Christian of the coming of Him Who is the Light of the World. The physical light is but an icon or image of Christ. Thus, the Christian begins the day by praising God for the dawn of the physical light as well as for the Light of the World which shines brightly in the face of Jesus. We pray that His light will guide us and show us the way for the day, blessing also the works of our hands which begin daily at this hour.

Abbreviated Prayers from the First Hour

Come, let us adore our God and King!

Come, let us adore Christ, our God and King!

Come, let us adore and fall down before the same
Lord Jesus Christ, our God and King!

Psalm 5

Give ear to my words, O Lord; give heed to
my groaning.

Harken to the sound of my cry, my King
and my God, for to You do I pray.

O Lord, in the morning You hear my voice;
in the morning I prepare a sacrifice for
You and watch.

For You are not a God who delights in
wickedness; evil may not sojourn with You.

The boastful may not stand before Your
eyes; You hate all evildoers.

You destroy those who speak lies; the Lord
abhors bloodthirsty and deceitful men.

But I through the abundance of Your
steadfast love will enter Your house, I
will worship toward Your holy temple
in fear of You.

Lead me, O Lord, in Your righteousness
because of my enemies; make Your way
straight before me.

For there is no truth in their mouth; their
heart is destruction, their throat is an
open sepulcher, they flatter with their
tongue.

Make them bear their guilt, O God; let them
fall by their own counsels; because of
their many transgressions cast them out,
for they have rebelled against You.

But let all who take refuge in You rejoice,
let them ever sing for joy; and defend
them, that those who love Your name
may exult in You.

For You bless the righteous, O Lord; You
cover him with favor as with a shield.

Prayer
Lord, Lord,
both day and night belong to you,
you formed the light and the sun
and marked the bounds of the earth.
And so we pray:
let your great mercy
shine on our wretchedness
like the dawning light;
free us from darkness
and from the shadow of death,
and from all the attacks and snares
of the evil one.

For we proclaim
the glory and holiness of Your Name,
worthy of all honour and majesty,
Father, Son and Holy Spirit,
now and forever,
to the ages of ages.

AMEN

Closing Prayer

Through the prayers of our holy Fathers, Lord
Jesus Christ, have mercy upon us and save us.

AMEN

The Third Hour

*All of them were filled with the Holy Spirit
and began to speak in other tongues...
(it was) only nine in the morning.*

ACTS 2: 4,15

The third hour (three hours after sunrise or 9:00
a.m.), was the exact time the Holy Spirit descended
upon the apostles on the day of Pentecost (ACTS 2:15).
This single theme dominates the third hour. One of
the three psalms that are read is the 51st which contains petitions for the sending of the Holy Spirit:
"Create in me a clean heart, O God; and renew a
right spirit within me...take not thy holy spirit from
me...and uphold me with thy free spirit" (Ps. 51:10-12).

Special prayers are said to thank God for sending the Holy Spirit on Pentecost, beseeching Him also to bestow the gift of the Spirit's presence upon us for the works of that day. The third hour is a daily reminder that the life of the faithful Christian remains empty without the inner presence of the Spirit. He is the One Who provides inner peace and power. He is the One "in Whom we live and move and have our being" (ACTS 17:28).

Abbreviated Prayers from the Third Hour

Come, let us adore our God and King!
Come, let us adore Christ, our God and King!
Come, let us adore and fall down before the
    same Lord Jesus Christ, our God and King!

King David's Confession (from Psalm 51)

Have mercy on me, O God
according to your unfailing love;
according to Your great compassion
blot out my transgressions.
Wash away all my iniquity
and cleanse me from my sin.
For I know my transgressions,
and my sin is always before me.
Against You, You only, have I sinned
and done what is evil in Your sight,
so that You are proved right when You speak
and justified when You judge.

Surely, I have been a sinner from birth,
sinful from the time my mother conceived me.
Surely You desire truth in the inner parts;
You teach me wisdom in the inmost place.
Create in me a pure heart, O God,
and renew a steadfast spirit within me.
Do not cast me from Your presence
or take Your Holy Spirit from me.
Restore to me the joy of your salvation
and grant me a willing spirit, to sustain me.
Then I will teach transgressors Your ways
and sinners will turn back to You.

Prayer
O God,
You have graciously brought us
to this hour,
the time when You poured out
Your Holy Spirit
in tongues of fire
upon Your apostles,
filling them with the gift
of Your grace;
so, most wonderful Lord,
may we too receive this blessing;
and as we seek to praise You,
merciful God,
in psalms and hymns and spiritual songs,
may we share in Your eternal Kingdom.

For Your Name
is worthy of all honour and majesty
and You are to be glorified in hymns of blessing,
Father, Son and Holy Spirit,
now and for ever,
to the ages of ages.

AMEN

Prayer
O Lord, You sent down Your Most Holy Spirit
upon Your apostles at the Third Hour.
Take Him not from us, O gracious One, but
renew us as we pray to You.

Closing Prayer
Through the prayers of our holy Fathers, Lord
Jesus Christ, have mercy upon us and save us.

AMEN

The Sixth Hour

> *There they crucified Him...It was now*
> *about the sixth hour.*

LK. 23:33, 34

The sixth hour, six hours following sunrise (noon),
coincides with the hour the Lord Jesus was crucified
(MATT. 27:45, LUKE 23:44, JOHN 19:14). Each day at noon the

Church tries to focus our attention on this great event in the history of our salvation. We offer Him prayers of gratitude for so loving each one of us that He gave His only begotten Son so that we who believe in Him may not perish but have life everlasting (JOHN 3:16). Our noontime prayers (sixth hour) include petitions that He save us from the sins and temptations of that day.

Abbreviated Prayers from the Sixth Hour

Come, let us adore our God and King!
Come, let us adore Christ, our God and King!
Come, let us adore and fall down before the
same Lord Jesus Christ, our God and King!

Psalm 54

Save me, O God, by Thy name,
and vindicate me by Thy might.
Hear my prayer, O God;
give ear to the words of my mouth.
For insolent men have risen against me,
ruthless men seek my life;
they do not set God before them.

SELAH

Behold, God is my helper;
the Lord is the upholder of my life,
He will requite my enemies with evil;
in Thy faithfulness put an end to them.

With a freewill offering I will sacrifice to Thee;
I will give thanks to Thy name, O Lord,
    for it is good.
For Thou hast delivered me from every trouble,
    and my eye has looked in triumph
    on my enemies.

Prayer
O Christ God, on the sixth day and hour,
    You nailed to the Cross the wrong which a
    rebellious Adam committed in paradise.
Destroy as well the record of our sins and save us!

✠ ✠ ✠ ✠ ✠

O Christ our God, who at this hour did stretch
    out Your loving arms upon the Cross
    that all might be gathered to You;
    help us and save us who sing to You:
Glory to Thee, O Lord.

✠ ✠ ✠ ✠ ✠

We bow low before Your most pure image,
O good One, begging You to forgive us our sins,
Christ our God! For You gladly ascended to the
cross in the flesh, of Your own free will, to free us
from satan's snares. For this, we thank You, Lord,
and we cry out to You:

By coming to save the world from sin, You have filled all things with joy!

✠ ✠ ✠ ✠ ✠

O Lord, Our God and King,
this was the hour
You stretched out undefiled hands
on the cross which we adore,
cancelling the record of our sins,
and nailing it to the cross:
remit now
every debt of sin
and set us free from the condemnation
which our evil thoughts, words or deeds deserve,
so that with pure hearts
we may at all times offer You
the worship that is Your due.

For to You belong
all glory, honour and praise,
Father, Son and Holy Spirit,
now and for ever,
to the ages of ages.   AMEN.

Closing Prayer
Through the prayers of our holy Fathers, Lord Jesus Christ, have mercy upon us and save us.

AMEN.

The Ninth Hour

> *And at the ninth hour...Jesus uttered a*
> *loud cry and breathed His last.*
>
> Mk. 15:34, 37

The ninth hour, nine hours following sunrise or 3:00 p.m., is the time when Jesus died on the cross. "And at about the ninth hour Jesus cried with a loud voice, saying, 'Eli, Eli, lama sabachthani?' That is to say, 'My God, my God, why hast thou forsaken me?'...When he had cried again with a loud voice (Jesus) yielded up the ghost" (Matthew 27:46, 50). At this time, prayers of thanksgiving are offered to Him Who by His death destroyed death. The prayers of the ninth hour conclude with a petition that we put to death the old sinful nature within us to enable us to live the new life in Christ Jesus with Whom we were not only crucified but also resurrected through baptism.

Abbreviated Prayers from the Ninth Hour

Come, let us adore our God and King!
Come, let us adore Christ, our God and King!
Come, let us adore and fall down before the
    same Lord Jesus Christ, our God and King!

Psalm 86

Incline Thy ear, O Lord, and answer me,
    for I am poor and needy.
Preserve my life, for I am godly;
    save Thy servant who trusts in Thee.
Thou art my God; be gracious to me,
    O Lord, for Thee do I cry all the day.
Gladden the soul by Thy servant,
    for to Thee, O Lord, do I lift up my soul.
For Thou, O Lord, art good and forgiving,
    abounding in steadfast love to all who
    call on Thee.
Give ear, O Lord, to my prayer;
    harken to my cry of supplication.
In the day of my trouble I call on Thee,
for Thou dost answer me.
There is none like Thee among the gods, O Lord,
    nor are there any works like Thine.
All the nations Thou hast made shall come
    and bow down before thee, O Lord,
    and shall glorify Thy name.
For Thou art great and doest wondrous things,
    Thou alone art God.
Teach me Thy way, O Lord,
    that I may walk in Thy truth;
    unite my heart to fear Thy name.
I give thanks to Thee, O Lord my
    God, with my whole heart,
    and I will glorify Thy name for ever.

For great is Thy steadfast love toward me;
    Thou hast delivered my soul from the
    depths of Sheol.

O God, insolent men have risen up against me;
    a band of ruthless men seek my life,
    and they do not set Thee before them.
But Thou, O Lord, art a God merciful and
    gracious, slow to anger and abounding
    in steadfast
    love and faithfulness.
Turn to me and take pity on me;
    give Thy strength to Thy servant,
    and save the son of Thy handmaid.
Show me a sign of Thy favor,
    that those who hate me may see
    and be put to shame
    because Thou, Lord, hast helped me
    and comforted me.

Prayers

O Master, Lord Jesus Christ, our God! Because of the patience with which You put up with our sinfulness, You have led us to this very hour when, suspended on the life-giving wood, You prepared for the thief the way into paradise and conquered death by death. Though we are not worthy of such graciousness, forgive us all the wrong we are guilty of. Our sinfulness is such that we dare not even lift our eyes to heaven, for we have abandoned the path of Your justice and preferred to crawl along the road of the obstinate willfulness of our own hearts! But now we entreat your boundless goodness: In your incomparable mercy, spare us; for Your name's sake, save us. Though we have spent our days in vanities of every sort, snatch us out of the hands of our foe and forgive us our sins. Deaden the cravings of our flesh, that we may discard the old man and put on the new, living only for You, our Master and Benefactor. By observing Your commandments, may we attain that eternal rest that all the blessed enjoy. For you are indeed the true happiness and joy of those who love You, Christ God, and we give You glory, together with Your eternal Father and Your all-holy, good, and life-giving Spirit: now and for ever, and unto ages of ages. AMEN.

✣✣✣✣✣

As Your flesh tasted death at the ninth hour, deal a death-blow to the cravings of our flesh, Christ our God, and save us!

The sight of life's very source suspended on the cross made the thief cry out: If this man who hangs with us were not God, the sun would never hide its light, nor would the earth so quake and tremble! O You who suffered all this, remember me, Lord, when You enter your kingdom!

Glory to the Father and the Son and the Holy Spirit

Planted there between two thieves, Your cross was like the balance for the scales of justice: For one thief perished from the sheer weight of his blasphemy, while the other rose out of his sinfulness through the recognition of your divinity. O Christ our God, glory to You!

Both now...

The Saviour of the world, at once both Lamb and Shepherd, was fixed upon the cross. Tearfully, his mother exclaimed: The world may well rejoice at the sight of its redemption, but my heart burns to see Your pain on this cross.

Closing Prayer

Through the prayers of our holy Fathers, Lord Jesus Christ, have mercy upon us and save us.

AMEN.

Vespers

Morning and evening were always considered to be proper times for prayer. Worship services were held every morning and evening in the Temple of Jerusalem and were continued by the early Christians even after they separated themselves from the worship of the Temple. The old Jewish psalms are still used. The theme of vespers takes us through creation, sin and salvation in Christ. It includes thanksgiving for the day now coming to an end and God's protection for the evening. In the Orthodox Church the liturgical day begins in the evening with the setting of the sun. The coming of darkness reminds us of the darkness of our sin and death and makes us long for the light. One of the great themes of vespers is the coming of Christ the Light to dispel the darkness. Jesus is praised as "The gladsome light of the holy glory of the Immortal Father" and "a light for revelation to the Gentiles." Vesper services are offered daily in monasteries and usually only on Saturday evenings in parishes. Evening prayers may be offered in private by Orthodox Christians daily by praying the Psalter and the other vesper prayers at home.

(SEE SECTION ON EVENING PRAYERS IN THIS BOOK).

The Midnight Office

The hour of midnight was designated as a time for prayer for three reasons. First, the Jewish people were led out of Egypt at midnight (Exodus 12:29). In remembrance of this event, the Messiah at the time of Jesus was expected to come at midnight. This expectation was fulfilled when Jesus was resurrected in the early morning while it was still dark (Matthew 28:1). Midnight also became associated in early Christian thought with the hour of the Second Coming of Jesus (Mark 13:35). He was expected to come "as a thief in the night" (1 Thess. 5:2,4). This hour of prayer is kept today only in certain monasteries where monks rise at midnight, as if from the grave of death, to meet the risen Lord in prayer. The prayers offered at this hour remember those who have died in Christ and also invoke God's mercy upon us for the coming judgement. Although we do not live in monasteries, we may use midnight as an hour of prayer if we happen to waken during the night. Instead of counting sheep, we can use the time to speak and pray to the Shepherd of our souls.

Praying the Hours Today

The service of the hours was not able to survive outside the monastic environment. People simply did not have the time to flock to the monasteries three or four times a day. Yet how much we need the inspiration and the power that comes to us today from the prayerful observance of these hours:

the FIRST HOUR: 7:00 a.m., to thank Jesus for the physical and spiritual light as a new day dawns;

the THIRD HOUR: 9:00 a.m., the hour of Pentecost, to thank God for the Holy Spirit beseeching Him for the Spirit's presence with us throughout the day;

the SIXTH HOUR: noon, to pause at that, the moment of His crucifixion, to thank Him for His great love for us;

the NINTH HOUR: 3:00 p.m., to remember him Who expired in our behalf at that very hour, repeating the words of the dying thief: "Remember me, Lord, when You come into your kingdom."

the TWELFTH HOUR: 6:00 p.m., to remember Him Who came to be "a light for revelation to the Gentiles."

the MIDNIGHT HOUR: to remember Him Who will come again as "a thief in the night" to judge the living and the dead.

The Trisagion Prayer

In the name of the Father and of the Son and of the Holy Spirit. AMEN.

Glory to You, our God. Glory to You.

O Heavenly King, the Comforter, the Spirit of Truth: You are everywhere filling all things; Treasury of blessings and Giver of Life: come and abide in us, and cleanse us from every impurity, and save our souls, O Good One!

Holy God! Holy Mighty! Holy Immortal! Have mercy on us.

Holy God! Holy Mighty! Holy Immortal! Have mercy on us.

Holy God! Holy Mighty! Holy Immortal! Have mercy on us.

Glory to the Father and to the Son and the the Holy Spirit, now and ever unto ages of ages. AMEN.

O Most Holy Trinity, have mercy on us!
O Lord, cleanse us from our sins!
O Master, pardon our transgressions!
O Holy One, visit and heal our infirmities for Your Name's sake.

Lord, have mercy.
Lord, have mercy.
Lord, have mercy.

Glory to the Father and to the Son and to the Holy Spirit, now and ever and unto ages of ages. AMEN.

Our Father, Who art in heaven, hallowed be Thy Name. Thy Kingdom come. Thy will be done, on earth as it is in heaven. Give us this day our daily bread; and forgive us our trespasses, as we forgive those who trespass against us; and lead us not into temptation, but deliver us from the evil one.

For Thine is the Kingdom and the power and the glory, of the Father and the Son and of the Holy Spirit, now and ever and unto ages of ages. AMEN.

Prayers Before and After Meals

Before Meals

In the name of the Father, and of the Son, and of the Holy Spirit. AMEN.

Our Father, Who art in Heaven, hallowed by Thy name. Thy kingdom come. Thy will be done, on earth as it is in Heaven. Give us this day our daily bread; and forgive us our trespasses, as we forgive those who trespass against us; and lead us not into temptation, but deliver us from evil.

Glory to the Father, and to the Son, and to the Holy Spirit, now and ever and unto the ages of ages. AMEN.

Lord, have mercy. (three times)

Christ our God, bless the food and drink of Your servants, for You are holy always, now and forever and to the ages of ages. AMEN.

Lord, Jesus Christ, our God,
who blessed the five loaves in the wilderness,
from which five thousand were fed,
bless also these loaves, this oil, this wine,

and all the fruits of the earth;
multiply them in this city, in this country,
and everywhere in Your world;
sanctify Your faithful who will receive them.
For You are the One who blesses
and feeds and sanctifies all creation,
O Christ our God,
and to You we give glory,
together with Your eternal Father
and Your all-holy, good and life creating Spirit,
now and ever and unto ages of ages. AMEN.

After Meals

We thank You, Christ our God, for You have satisfied us with earthly gifts. Do not deprive us of Your heavenly kingdom, but as You, O Savior, came among Your disciples and gave them peace, come among us also and save us.

Glory to the Father, and to the Son, and to the Holy Spirit, now and ever and unto ages of ages. AMEN.

Lord, have mercy. (Three times)
Blessed is God, who has mercy on us and nourishes us from His bountiful gifts by His grace and compassion always, now and ever and unto the ages of ages. AMEN.

Prayer Before and After Reading God's Word

In the Orthodox Church we cherish the highest respect for the Bible. The Gospel book is kept enthroned on the altar constantly. Just as the Bible is enthroned on the altar of the Church, so it should be enthroned in the mind and heart of every Orthodox Christian. By this we don't mean that it should be kept on some shelf at home as a magic charm. It should be opened and read daily.

We offer the following suggestions for family Bible reading:

• Set aside a regular time for daily reading, preferably in the evening at the supper table when the whole family is together. When the children are young, mom or dad can do the reading. When the children grow older, they may share in the reading. Reading to children is one of life's greatest joys. Children treasure it.

• Don't read too much or too fast. One chapter a day is sufficient. Let what you read sink in slowly. If the children are young, read from a Bible story book–one that has pictures which you can show the children.

- Start with the Gospels of Jesus (MATTHEW, MARK, LUKE AND JOHN).

- Read prayerfully with the faith and the expectation that God will really and truly speak to you through what you read.

- Don't worry about the passages you do not understand. Concentrate on what you do understand. The more you read, the more you will understand. One passage explains another.

- Each day memorize at least one verse that grips you. Say it out loud as a family three or four times. Encourage your children to fall asleep with this verse on their lips. Write it in a notebook.

- As you read, try to have an icon of Jesus before you if you are reading the Gospels; one of St. Paul if you are reading his epistles, etc. This will help you realize who it is who is speaking to you.

- Purchase a copy of "The Orthodox Study Bible," read the Lectionary which has the daily Scripture readings for each day. Also read the sections on "How to Read the Bible," "How to Read the New Testament in a Year," and "Interpreting the Scriptures."

- Seek God's help in applying the truths you read to your life.

- If you have any questions about what you have read, seek advice from your priest.

Prayer Before Reading the Bible

*In the name of the Father and the Son and
the Holy Spirit. Amen.*

Shine into our hearts, O loving Master, the pure light of Your divine knowledge and open the eyes of our minds to an understanding of the things Your Gospel teaches. Implant in us also a reverence for Your blessed commandments so that, putting down the desires of our bodies, we may pursue a spiritual way of life, thinking and doing only those things that will please You. For You are the light of our souls and our bodies, Christ our God and to You we give glory, Father, Son and Holy Spirit, now and forever and to the endless ages.

–FROM THE LITURGY OF ST. JOHN CHRYSOSTOM

Thanksgiving Following Bible Reading

O how I love Your law!
It is my meditation all the day.
Your word is a lamp to my feet
and a light to my path.

PSALM 119:97, 105

O God, You have spoken to us your divine and
saving words.
Illumine the souls of us sinners
to comprehend that which has been read,
that we do not appear simply
          as hearers of your spiritual words,
          but doers of good deeds,
          true pursuers of faith,
          having a blameless life
          and a conduct without reproach
in Christ our Lord,
with whom You are blessed and glorified,
together with Your all-holy and good, and
life-giving Spirit,
now and forever and to the ages of ages.

PRAYER FROM THE LITURGY OF ST. JAMES

The Jesus Prayer

BY FR. LEV GILLET

Lord Jesus Christ, Son of God, have
mercy on me the sinner.

1.   The invocation of the Name of Jesus can be put to
     many frames. It is for each person to find the form
     which is the most appropriate to his or her own
     prayer. But, whatever formula may be used, the
     heart and centre of the invocation must be the
     Holy Name itself, the word *Jesus*. There resides
     the whole strength of the invocation.

2. The Name of Jesus may either be used alone or be inserted in a more or less developed phrase. In the East the commonest form is: "Lord Jesus Christ, Son of God, have mercy on me the sinner." One might simply say, "Jesus Christ," or "Lord Jesus." The invocation may even be reduced to one single word, "Jesus."

3. This last form–the Name of Jesus only–is the most ancient mould of the invocation of the Name. It is the shortest, the simplest and, as we think, the easiest. Therefore, without deprecating the other formulas, we suggest that the word "Jesus" alone should be used.

4. Thus, when we speak of the invocation of the Name, we mean the devout and frequent repetition of the Name itself, of the word "Jesus" without additions. The Holy Name is the prayer.

5. The Name of Jesus may be either pronounced or silently thought. In both cases there is a real invocation of the Name, verbal in the first case, and purely mental in the second. This prayer affords an easy transition from verbal to mental prayer. Even the verbal repetition of the Name, if it is slow and thoughtful, makes us pass to mental prayer and disposes the soul to contemplation.

Morning Prayers

Waking up in the morning can be a vital spiritual experience. It can be a reminder of that "great gettin' up morning" when the the Lord will appear and will raise me from my grave to live with Him forever. Thus, as I rise from bed every morning may I visualize my rising from the tomb at the coming of my Lord and going up to meet Him in the clouds. I rise every morning to meet Him, if not in the clouds, certainly in the experiences and events of the day, to walk with Him, talk with Him, love, obey and serve Him in all that I do that day.

When Jesus appeared to His disciples after the Resurrection, He said, "Come, let us have breakfast" (JOHN 21). The Church invites us daily to have "breakfast with Jesus," who is the Bread of Life, through the following prayers.

Begin with the Trisagion Prayers (see page 29).

✚✚✚✚✚

O Lord, grant that we may meet the coming day in peace.
Help us in all things to rely upon Your holy will.
In each hour of the day, reveal Your will to us.

Bless our dealings with all who surround us.
Teach us to treat all that shall come to us throughout the day with peace of soul, and with the firm conviction that Your will governs all.
In all our deeds and words, guide our thoughts and feelings.
In unforseen events, let us not forget that all are sent by You.
Teach us to act firmly and wisely, without embittering and embarrassing others.
Give us the strength to bear the fatigue of the coming day, with all that it shall bring.

Direct our wills.
Teach us to pray.
Pray within us. AMEN.

✤ ✤ ✤ ✤ ✤

Most holy God, we pray and beseech You, give each of us a pure heart and a way of speaking that befits the faith we profess; grant us uprightness of purpose, powers of reasoning unhindered by passions, conduct that becomes those who fear You, and perfect knowledge of Your commandments; may we enjoy health in body and in spirit.

Grant us a life of peace, genuine faith and living hope, sincere charity and bountiful generosity, patience that knows no bounds and the light of Your truth to proclaim Your goodness to us, that for ever and in all things placing our trust only in You, we may abound in every good work, and that in Christ Your gifts may increase in every soul.

For to You belong all glory, honor and majesty, Father, Son and Holy Spirit, now and ever and unto ages of ages. AMEN.

A Morning Prayer From the Daily Hours

Since the darkest hour
our souls have kept their watch before You,
O Lord our God,
for Your commandments are light
to the earth.
Teach us, O God,
Your righteousness, Your precepts and Your wisdom.
Enlighten our minds
that we not slumber in the sin
that leads to death.
Put far from our hearts all darkness,
but give us the sun of your righteousness,
and may the seal of Your Holy Spirit
keep us from all harm.
Direct our feet in the way of peace,
let us greet the dawn
and the new day with gladness,
and offer You our morning prayers.

For Yours is the greatness,
the majesty, the power and the glory,
Father, Son and Holy Spirit,
now and for ever
to the ages of ages. AMEN.

Prayers from the Psalms

"But Thou, O Lord, art a shield about me,
my glory, and the lifter of my head.
I cry aloud to the Lord,
and He answers me from His holy hill.

I lie down and sleep;
I wake again, for the Lord,
sustains me.
I am not afraid of ten thousands
of people
Who have set themselves against
me round about   (Ps. 3:3-6).

✠ ✠ ✠ ✠ ✠

O Lord, in the morning Thou dost
hear my voice;
In the morning I prepare a
sacrifice for Thee, and watch.   (Ps. 5:3)

✠ ✠ ✠ ✠ ✠

But I call upon the Lord;
and the Lord will save me.
Evening, morning and at noon
I utter my complaint and moan,
and He will hear my voice.   (Ps. 55:16-17)

✤ ✤ ✤ ✤ ✤

But I, O Lord, cry to Thee;
in the morning my prayer comes
before Thee.   (Ps. 88:13)

✤ ✤ ✤ ✤ ✤

It is good to give thanks to the Lord,
to sing praises to Thy name,
O Most High;
to declare Thy steadfast love in the
morning,
and Thy faithfulness by night,

to the music of the lute and the harp,
For thou, O Lord, hast made me
glad by thy work;
at the works of Thy hands I sing
for joy.   (Ps. 92:1-2)

✤ ✤ ✤ ✤ ✤

Let me hear in the morning of Thy
steadfast love,
for in Thee I put my trust.
Teach me the way I should go,
for to Thee I lift up my soul.

Deliver me, O Lord, from my
enemies!
I have fled to Thee for refuge!
Teach me to do Thy will, for Thou art my God!
Let Thy good spirit lead me
on a level path!   (Ps. 143-8:10)

✠ ✠ ✠ ✠ ✠

This is the day which the Lord has made
let us rejoice and be glad in it.   (Ps. 118:24)

✠ ✠ ✠ ✠ ✠

Daily Bible Reading

Please refer to the Lectionary in the back of "The
Orthodox Study Bible" for the appointed Bible
readings for each day.

A Morning Prayer by the Elders of Optino

O Lord, grant that I may meet all that this coming
day brings to me with spiritual tranquility. Grant

that I may fully surrender myself to Your holy Will.

At every hour of this day, direct and support me in all things. Whatsoever news may reach me in the course of the day, teach me to accept it with a calm soul and the firm conviction that all is subject to Your holy Will.

Direct my thoughts and feelings in all my words and actions. In all unexpected occurrences, do not let me forget that all is sent down from You.

Grant that I may deal straightforwardly and wisely with every member of my family, neither embarrassing nor saddening anyone.

O Lord, grant me the strength to endure the fatigue of the coming day and all the events that take place. Direct my will and teach me to pray, to believe, to hope, to be patient, to forgive and to love. AMEN.

And this prayer:
In rising from sleep to begin another day, O Holy Trinity, Father, Son and Holy Spirit, I give thanks to You for being so patient with me in Your great goodness, for never showing any anger with me in spite of my failings and laziness, and for refusing

to let me perish in my sins. Instead, You have shown me Your great love for mankind over and over again, raising me up from every new trouble I fall into, that again and again I might cry out to You with each new day, praising Your almighty power. Enlighten the eyes of my mind and heart and open my lips to ponder and reflect on Your word, to come to an understanding of Your commandments, to do Your will in all things, and to sing to You from the depths of my heart, forever glorifying your most holy name, Father, Son and Holy Spirit; now and forever more. AMEN.

✝ ✝ ✝ ✝ ✝

Morning Prayer

We give Thee hearty thanks for the rest of the past night, and for the gift of a new day, with its opportunities of pleasing Thee. Grant that we may so pass its hours in the perfect freedom of Thy service, that at eventide we may again give thanks unto thee; through Jesus Christ our Lord. AMEN.   THIRD CENTURY

The Breastplate Prayer

I bind unto myself today
The power of God to hold and lead,
His eye to watch, His might to stay,
His ear to hearken to my need.

The wisdom of my God to teach,
His hand to guide, His shield to ward;
The word of God to give me speech,
His heavenly host to be my guard.

Christ, be with me, Christ before me,
    Christ behind me,
Christ in me, Christ beneath me,
    Christ above me,
Christ on my right, Christ on my left
Christ when I lie, Christ when I sit,
Christ when I arise,
Christ in the heart of every one who
    thinks of me.
Christ in the mouth of every one who
    speaks of me,
Christ in every eye that sees me.
Christ in every ear that hears me.
    Salvation is of the Lord,
    Salvation is of the Christ,
    May your salvation, O Lord, be ever with us.

ST. PATRICK

A Child's Morning Prayer

Lord Jesus, thank you for the bright sunlight of a
    new day.
As You made the sun to rise in the heavens, so
    come to shine in my life today.
For You are the Light of the world.

Guide me, direct me, lead me that I may do
    Your holy will and please You
    in all that I do this day.
Bless my parents, teachers and all who care
    for me. AMEN.

Personal Prayer Requests

Always allow time to bring your personal concerns and requests to the Lord. Let each person in the family share in this by using petitions such as: "Let us pray for...." mentioning specific people. "Let us thank God for....". "Let us ask God's forgiveness for....", etc.

✢ ✢ ✢ ✢ ✢

In the evening, morning and noontime,
we praise You, we bless You,
we give thanks to You,
and we pray to You, O Master of all,
O Lord who loves humankind.
Guide our prayers aright
as an offering of sweet incense before You;
let not our heart incline to words or thoughts of wickedness,
but save us from all dangers
and from the evil powers that pursue our souls.
For to You, O Lord,
are our eyes directed,

and in You have we hoped.
Let us not be put to shame.
For to You belong all glory, honour and worship,
to the Father and to the Son and the Holy Spirit,
now and forever. AMEN.

LITURGY OF THE PRESANCTIFIED GIFTS

We bless You, O God, most high and Lord of
mercy,
You are always doing great and inscrutable things
with us, glorious and wonderful, and without
number.
You grant us sleep for rest from our infirmities,
and repose from the burdens of our much-toiling
flesh.
We thank You, for You have not destroyed us with
our sins,
but have continued to love us;
and though we were sunk in despair,
You have raised us up to glorify Your power.
Therefore, we implore Your incomparable
goodness.

Enlighten the eyes of our understanding,
and raise up our minds
from the heavy sleep of indolence.
Open our mouth and fill it with Your praise,
that we may be able without distraction
to sing and to confess that You are God,

glorified in all and by all,
the eternal Father, with Your only begotten Son,
and Your all holy, good and life-giving Spirit,
now and forever and to the ages of ages.
AMEN.

St. Basil the Great, 4th century

✛ ✛ ✛ ✛ ✛

O Lord, keep us this day without sin.
Blessed are you, O Lord,
God of our fathers and mothers,
and your name is praised and glorified for ever.

Let Your mercy come upon us, O Lord,
even as we set our hope on You.
Blessed are You, O Lord,
even as we have set our hope on You.
Blessed are You, O Lord,
teach me Your statutes.
Blessed are You, O Master,
make me to understand Your statutes.
Blessed are You, O Master,
make me to understand Your statutes.
Blessed are You, O Holy one,
enlighten me with Your statutes.
Your mercy, O Lord, is for ever.
Do not overlook the works of Your hands.
To You belongs praise;

to You is due song;
to You is due glory;
to the Father, and to the Son, and the Holy Spirit
now and always, and to the ages of ages. AMEN.

MATINS

✤ ✤ ✤ ✤ ✤

O Lord, Jesus Christ my God, forsake me not.
O Lord, do not stand afar off from me.
O Lord, stretch out to me a helping hand.
O Lord, support me with the fear of You.
O Lord, plant this fear and the love for You
in my heart.
O Lord, teach me to do Your will.

ST. PAISIOS THE GREAT, 4TH CENTURY

✤ ✤ ✤ ✤ ✤

As I rise up out of the dark,
O lover of humankind,
I beseech You,
enlighten and guide me also
in Your commandments,
and teach me to always do Your will.

MATINS HYMN

✤ ✤ ✤ ✤ ✤

Our spirit seeks You in the early dawn, O God,
for Your commandments are light.
Teach us, O Master, Your righteousness
and make us worthy to follow Your
commandments with all our strength.
Take away from our hearts every darkness.
Grant to us the Sun of righteousness
and protect our lives from any bad influence
with the seal of Your most Holy Spirit.
Direct our steps to the way of peace
and grant to us that this present morning may be
peaceful so that we may send up the morning
hymns,
to You the Father and the Son and the Holy
Spirit, the only God,
who is without beginning
and creator of all. AMEN.

ST. BASIL THE GREAT, 4TH CENTURY

The Office of Holy Matins
(Abbreviated)

The Trisagion Prayer (see p. 39)

Having arisen from sleep, we fall down before You, O
Blessed One,

and sing to You, O Mighty one, the Angelic Hymn:

Holy, holy, holy are You, O God. Through the Theotokos have mercy on us.

Glory be to the Father, and to the Son, and the Holy Spirit: From my bed and sleep You have raised me: O Lord, enlighten my mind and my heart, and open my lips that I may praise You, O Holy Trinity: Holy, holy, holy are You, O God. Through the Theotokos have mercy on us.

Both now and always and for ever and ever. Amen. Suddenly the Judge shall come, and the deeds of each shall be revealed; but with fear we cry out in the middle of the night: Holy, holy, holy are You, O God. Through the Theotokos have mercy on us.

The Lord is God, and He has appeared to us. Blessed is He who comes in the name of the Lord.

Let us complete our morning prayer to the Lord. Help us, save us, have mercy on us and protect us, O God, by Your grace.

That this whole day may be perfect, holy, peaceful and without sin, let us ask the Lord.

For an angel of peace, a faithful guide and guardian of our souls and bodies, let us ask the Lord.

For the forgiveness and remission of our sins and offenses, let us ask the Lord.

For what is good and profitable to our souls and for peace in the world, let us ask the Lord.

That the rest of our life may be spent in peace and repentance, let us ask the Lord.

That the end of our life may be Christian, painless, unashamed and peaceful, and for a good defense before the awesome judgement seat of Christ, let us ask the Lord.

Let us remember our all holy, spotless, most highly blessed and glorious Lady, the Mother of God and ever-virgin Mary, with all the saints, and commend ourselves and one another and our whole life to Christ our God.

For You are the God of mercy, of compassion and love for mankind, and we send up glory to You, Father, Son and Holy Spirit, now and always and for ever and ever.

The Doxology (see page 142)

Scripture Reading

The Creed

I Believe in one God, Father Almighty, Creator of heaven and earth and of all things visible and invisible. And in one Lord Jesus Christ, the only begotten Son of God, begotten of the Father before all ages: Light of light, true God of true God, begotten not made, of one substance with the Father, by whom all things were made; who for us all and for our Salvation came down from heaven, and was incarnate of the Holy Spirit and the Virgin Mary, and was made man; who was crucified for us under Pontius Pilate, and suffered, and was buried; who rose again on the third day in accordance with the Scriptures, and ascended into heaven, and is enthroned at the right hand of the Father; who will come again with glory to judge the living and the dead; and of whose kingdom there shall be no end. And in the Holy Spirit, the Lord, the Giver of Life, who proceeds from the Father, who together with the Father and the Son is worshiped and glorified; who spoke through the prophets. In one, holy catholic and apostolic Church. I profess one baptism for the remission of sins. I look forward to the resurrection of the dead and the life of the world to come. Amen.

✚✚✚✚✚

O God, in the night my soul awakens early to You, for Your laws are a light. Teach me Your righteousness, Your commandments and Your statutes, O God. Enlighten the eyes of my understanding that I may not sleep to death in sins. Remove all darkness from my heart. Graciously give me the Sun of Righteousness, and preserve my life unassailed, by the seal of your Holy Spirit. Guide my steps in the way of peace. Grant me to behold the dawn and the day with joy, that I may offer my morning prayer to you. For Yours is the dominion, and Yours is the majesty and the power and the glory; + of the Father, and the Son, and the Holy Spirit: now and ever, and to ages of ages. AMEN.

Evening Prayers

These prayers may be offered just before retiring or at the table following the evening meal with your spouse and children.

First say the TRISAGION PRAYERS (see page 29), and then the following:

Now that the day has come to a close, I thank You, Lord, and I pray that the evening with the night be without sin. Grant this to me, Savior, and save me.

Glory to the Father, and to the Son, and to the Holy Spirit.

Now that the day has ended, I glorify You, O Master, and I pray that I pass the evening and the night without sin. Grant this to me, O Savior, and save me.

Now and forever. Amen.

Now that the day has run its course, I praise You, O Holy One, and I pray that the evening with the night may be peaceful and undisturbed. Grant this to me, O Savior, and save me.

Lord have mercy (3 times).

Prayers of Forgiveness
O Lord our God, if during this day I have sinned, whether in word or deed or thought, forgive me all, for You are good and love mankind. (At this point acknowledge and confess to God specific personal sins).

Grant me peaceful and undisturbed sleep, and deliver me from the temptations of the evil one.

Raise me up again in the morning that I may glorify You; for You are blessed: with Your Only-begotten

Son and Your All-holy Spirit: now and forevermore. AMEN.

✚ ✚ ✚ ✚ ✚

O Lord our God, forgive all the sins I have committed this day in word, deed and thought, for You are good and love mankind. Grant me a peaceful sleep, free of restlessness. Send Your Guardian Angel to protect and keep me from all harm. For You are the Guardian of our souls and bodies, and to You we ascribe glory, to the Father, and to the Son, and to the Holy Spirit, now and forevermore. AMEN.

✚ ✚ ✚ ✚ ✚

In All Seasons And In Every Hour
O Christ our God, You are worshiped at all times and in all places and are glorified both in heaven and on earth. You are patient, generous in mercy, rich in compassion, loving to the just and merciful to the sinner. You call all of us to repentance through the promise of blessings to come.

O Lord, receive our supplications at this very hour. Direct our lives in the way of Your commandments. Sanctify our souls, purify our bodies, set our minds aright, cleanse our thoughts, deliver us from all affliction, wrath, danger and need. Surround us with Your holy angels, so that, guided and guarded by their ranks, we may reach unity of the faith and the knowledge of Your unutterable glory. You are blessed unto ages of ages. AMEN.

A Prayer of Intercession

Lord, we pray for peace in the world.
For all the faithful and Orthodox Christians.
For our Archbishop (name), our Bishop (name), and all our brothers and sisters in Christ.
For our nation, our president, and all those in the service of our country.
For our parents, our brothers and sisters,
    our relatives and friends.
For those who hate us and those who love us.
For those who work with us and those who serve us.
For those who have asked us to pray for them.
For travelers by land, sea and air.
For prisoners and captives.
For those who are hungry, suffering, and the sick
For those departed from this life in the hope of resurrection.

Personal Prayer Requests

Let each person in the family participate by using petitions such as: "Let us pray for...." mentioning specific names. "Let us thank God for...". "Let us ask forgiveness for..." etc.

A Child's Evening Prayer

Dearest Jesus, I am one of Your children.
Take me into Your arms and bless me
as You embraced children
when You visited us on earth.
Hear my prayer this evening.
May Your icon which I keep by my bedside
Ever remind me that while I
sleep, You are always with me.
Make me sleep in peace and let
me awaken in the morning
to love You and serve You. Amen.

✠ ✠ ✠ ✠ ✠

Daily Bible Readings

Refer to the Lectionary in back of "The Orthodox
Study Bible" for the Bible readings assigned to this
day.

From the Prayer of the Hours (Vespers)

Blessed are You, O God, Almighty Lord,
who made the sun to give light to the day
and brightened the night with the shining stars:
You have brought us through this long day
and lead us to the threshold of night;
hear our prayer
and the prayers of your people,
forgive us all

the sins we have committed deliberately or
    in our weakness,
receive our evening supplications,
and pour out upon your inheritors
the riches of your goodness and mercy.
Set your holy angels round about us,
clothe us in the armor of righteousness,
strengthen us with your truth
and defend us with your power;
deliver us from every attack of the devil
who seeks to ensnare us.
Grant that this evening
and the night to come
and all the days of our life
may pass in holiness and peace,
without our falling into sin or error
and untroubled by apparitions and beguiling influences,
through the mediation of the holy Mother of God
and all the saints
who have found favour with You since time began.
For You indeed, O Lord our God,
have mercy on us and save us, and we glorify You,
Father, Son and Holy Spirit,
now and for ever,
to the ages of ages. Amen.

Evening Prayer

Watch, dear Lord,
with those who wake, or watch, or weep tonight,
and give Your angels charge over those who sleep.
Tend Your sick ones, O Lord, Christ,
rest Your weary ones.
Bless Your dying ones
Soothe Your suffering ones.
Pity Your afflicted ones.
Shield Your joyous ones.
And all for Your love's sake.
AMEN.   ST. AUGUSTINE

✠ ✠ ✠ ✠ ✠

May my prayer be set before you
like incense;
may the lifting up of my hands be like the
evening sacrifice. Psalm 141:2

Prayer to the Theotokos

O all-pure and incorruptible Virgin Bride of God, and
our Sovereign Lady, who made the Word of God one
with mankind by gloriously giving birth to your Son
and joining our fallen nature to His divine nature;
who are the hope of the despairing and the support of
those in distress, the swift defender of those who turn
to you and the refuge of all Christians:

Do not turn from me, an unclean sinner, who have destroyed myself with unworthy thoughts, words and deeds, and have been enslaved by forgetfulness to the carnal passions of life; but have compassion on me, O Theotokos, and accept the prayer of a sinner and prodigal, offered from unclean lips.

Exercise your boldness as a mother, and pray to your Son, our Lord and Master, that He will make known to me also His compassionate goodness, and overlooking my countless sins, will turn me to repentance and make me fervent in doing His commandments.

Be with me always in your grace and loving mercy, for you are the fervent helper who turns away the assaults of enemies and guides all toward salvation, caring for my unworthy soul at the hour of death and driving from it the darkness of evil spirits. In the Day of Judgment, free me from eternal torment and show me to be an heir of the divine glory of your Son, and our God.

Grant this, O Lady Theotokos, by your prayers and intercessions, through the mercy and lovingkindness of Your only begotten Son, our Lord and Savior Jesus Christ, to Whom are due all glory, honor and worship, with the Father Who is eternal, and His all-holy, good and life-giving Spirit, now and ever and unto ages of ages. Amen.

Prayer to the Lord

And grant rest, O Master, to our souls and bodies as we sleep; preserve us from the gloomy slumber of sin and from the dark passions of the night. Calm the impulses of carnal desires, quench the fiery darts of the evil one which are craftily directed against us. Still the rebellions of the flesh, and put far from us all anxiety and worldly cares.

Grant us, O God, a watchful mind, pure thoughts, a sober heart and a quiet rest free from every vision of the devil. Raise us up again at the hour of prayer, strengthened in Your precepts and holding within us steadfastly the thought of Your commandments.
Grant that we may sing praises to You through the night and that we may hymn, bless and glorify Your all-honorable and majestic Name, of the Father and of the Son and of the Holy Spirit, now and ever and unto ages of ages. Amen.

To The Theotokos

O exceedingly glorious and ever-virgin Theotokos, bring our petitions before your Son, and our God, and implore Him that through you He will save our souls. Amen.

To The Holy Trinity

O Father, my hope!
O Son, my refuge!

O Holy Spirit, my protection!
O Most Holy Trinity: Glory to You!

O Gladsome Light

O gladsome Light of the holy glory of the immortal,
heavenly, holy, blessed Father: Jesus Christ!
Now that we have come to the setting of the sun and
behold the light of evening,
We praise God–Father, Son and Holy Spirit.
At all times, You are worthy of praise in song:
O Son of God and Giver of Life–
Therefore, all the world glorifies You!

Prayer of St. Simeon

(Luke 2:29-32)
Lord, now lettest Thou Thy servant depart in peace,
According to Thy word,
For mine eyes have seen Thy salvation,
Which Thou hast prepared before the face of
all people–
A Light to lighten the Gentiles
And the glory of Thy people Israel.

Vouchsafe, O Lord

Vouchsafe, O Lord, to keep us this night without sin.
Blessed are You, O Lord, the God of our fathers, and
praised and glorified is Your Name for ever. AMEN.

Let Your mercy be upon us, O Lord, even as we have set our hope on You.

Blessed are You, O Lord; teach me Your statutes.

Blessed are you, O Master; make me to understand Your commandments.

Blessed are You, O Holy One; enlighten me with Your precepts.

Your mercy endures for ever, O Lord! Do not despise the works of Your hands!

To You belongs worship, to You belongs praise, to You belongs glory: to the Father and to the Son and the Holy Spirit, now and ever and unto ages of ages. Amen.

Closing Prayer

Into Your hands, Lord Jesus Christ, I commend my soul and my body. Bless me, have mercy on me, and grant me life eternal. Amen.

Benediction

Through the prayers of our holy Fathers, O Lord Jesus Christ our Lord, have mercy on us and save us. Amen.

The Little Compline

Begin with the Trisagion Prayer (see page 29).

Psalm 51 (see page 15).

Psalm 70
O God, come to deliver me!
O Lord, make haste to help me!
Let them be put to shame and confusion
who seek my life!
Let them be turned back and brought
    dishonor
        who wish me evil!
Let them be turned back in shame
    who jeer at me, "Aha, Aha!"
May all who seek You
    rejoice and be glad in You!
May those who love Your salvation
    say evermore, "God is great!"
But I am poor and needy;
    hasten to me, O God!
You are my help and my deliverer;
    O Lord, do not delay!

Psalm 143
O Lord, hear my prayer; in Your truth give
    heed to my supplication!
In Your righteousness, hear me!

And enter not into judgement with
    Your servant;
for no one living is righteous in
    Your sight.

The enemy has pursued my soul;
    he has crushed my life to the ground;
he has made me dwell in darkness
    like those long dead.
Therefore my spirit faints within me;
    my heart within me is distressed.

I remembered the days of old,
    I meditated on all Your deeds;
    I thought of the works of Your hands.

I stretched out my hands to You;
    my soul longs for You like a
    parched land.
Make haste to answer me, O Lord!
My spirit fails!
Hide not Your face from me,
    lest I be like those who go down to
    the pit.
Let me hear in the morning of Your
    steadfast love.
    for in You I put my trust.
Teach me the way I should go,
    for to you I lift up my soul.

Deliver me, O Lord, from my enemies.
I have fled to You for refuge.
Teach me to do Your will,
    for You are my God!
Let Your good Spirit lead me on a
    level path.

For Your name's sake, O Lord,
    preserve my life.
In your righteousness bring me out
    of trouble.
And in your steadfast love cut off
    my enemies,
    and destroy all those who afflict my
    soul,
    for I am Your servant.

The Doxology (see page 142)

The Creed (see page 54)

The Magnificat (see page 141)

The Prayer to Jesus (see page 63)

The Prayer to the Theotokos (see page 61)

Prayers for Healing

O Lord our God, Who are righteous, compassionate, the Physician of our souls and bodies;
By whose stripes we are healed;
The Good Shepherd, who comes to search for the wandering sheep;
Who desires not the death of a sinner but that he may turn from his wickedness and live;
Who gives consolation to the faint-hearted and life to those who are shattered;
Who did heal the woman who had an issue of blood for twelve years;
Who did set free the daughter of the woman of Canaan, who was tormented by a devil;
Who did bestow healing and forgiveness of sins upon the paralytic;
Who did justify the publican by Your word, and accepted the thief through his confession at the last moment;
Who took the sins of the world and nailed them to the cross:
Lord, to You I lift up my voice:
Stretch forth Your powerful arm.
Send down from heaven Your healing power.
Touch my sick body.
Bless the means used for my recovery and those who administer them.
Release the fever.

Soothe the suffering.
Drive away the weakness.
Forgive my sins.
Raise me up from the bed of affliction.
Grant that this sickness may be the means of my repentance and transformation.
For I am but dust and if I live at all it is only by Your power and grace.
To You, Lord Jesus, I direct my prayer, and trusting in Your mercy and love, I offer all worship and adoration to You, and the eternal Father and the most Holy Spirit now and ever and unto ages of ages. Amen.

✠ ✠ ✠ ✠ ✠

O Lord Almighty,
the healer of our souls and bodies,
    You put down and raise up,
    You chastise and heal also;
visit now in Your great mercy
our brothers and sisters who are sick.
Stretch forth Your hand that is full of healing and health,
    and get them up from their bed,
    and cure them of their illness.
Put away from them the spirit of disease and of every malady,
    pain and fever to which they are bound;
and if they have sins and transgressions,

grant to them remission and forgiveness,
   since You love all your people.
Yes, Lord my God,
pity Your creation,
through the compassion of Your only-begotten Son,
together with Your all-holy, good and life-creating
Spirit,
with whom You are blessed,
both now and ever, and to the ages of ages. AMEN.

PRAYER FOR THE SICK

✠ ✠ ✠ ✠ ✠

Lord,
it was not the pool
that healed the paralytic, but Your word.
The power of Your voice
   was stronger than the chronic bond of the disease.
Therefore he cast away the burden of sickness
   and took up his bed
   as a witness to Your abundant mercies.
Lord, glory to You!

SUNDAY OF THE PARALYTIC

✠ ✠ ✠ ✠ ✠

O Lord our God,
who by word alone healed all diseases,
who cured the kinswoman of Peter,
You chastise with pity and heal according to Your

goodness,
You are able to put aside every malady and infirmity,
You are the same Lord,
grant aid to Your servants
and cure them of every sickness which grieves them;
lift them up from their bed of pain,
send down upon them your great mercy,
and if it be Your will,
give to them health and a complete recovery;
for You are the physician of our souls and bodies,
and to You we offer glory:
to the Father, and to the Son, and the Holy Spirit,
both now and ever , and to the ages of ages. AMEN.

PRAYER FOR THE SICK

✠✠✠✠✠

O Christ, who alone are our defender,
visit and heal Your suffering servants
delivering them from sickness and grievous pains.
Raise them up
    that they may sing to You
    and praise You without ceasing;
through the prayers of the Theotokos,
O You who alone loves mankind.

PRAYER FOR THE SICK

Thanksgiving for Recovery After Illness
Almighty God, our Heavenly Father,
Source of life and

Fountain of all good things,
I bless Your holy name, and
Offer You most hearty thanks
For having restored me to health.
Grant me Your continuing grace, I pray,
That I may persist in my desire to follow You
And correct the errors of my past life,
Improving in virtue and
Living a new life of faithful obedience and
Service to You,
That, thus living for You, I may be
Found ready when it pleases You
to call me to Your kingdom,
Where You dwell in glory with Your
only begotten Son, our Lord Jesus
Christ, and Your all-holy and
life-giving Spirit,
To whom are due all glory, honor,
worship and thanksgiving now
and forevermore. AMEN.

Prayer for Travel

Lord Jesus,
You who are the Way, the Truth, and the Life;
You who travelled with your servant Joseph;
You who accompanied Your two disciples on the road
to Emmaus

and set their hearts aflame with the warmth of Your love;

Travel with me also and bless my journey.

Warm and gladden my heart with the nearness of Your Presence.

Surround me with Your holy angels to keep me safe.

Deliver and protect me from all danger, misfortune and temptation.

Keep me in the center of Your love and obedient to Your will.

Journey always with me in my greater journey as a pilgrim on earth on my way home to You.

Help me return home again in peace, health and good will that I may praise and glorify Your exalted Name, Father, Son, and Holy Spirit all the days of my life. AMEN.

Prayers to the Holy Spirit

O Heavenly King,
Comforter,
the Spirit of truth,
present in all places and filling all things;
treasury of good things and giver of life,
come and dwell in us
and purify us from every stain,
and of Your goodness save our souls.

PRAYER TO HOLY SPIRIT

✤ ✤ ✤ ✤ ✤

O Holy Spirit, how dear You are to the soul!
Paradise is the kingdom of the Holy Spirit.
O Holy Spirit, live in our souls,
that with one accord we may all glorify the Creator:
Father, Son and Holy Spirit.

Starets Silouan

✤ ✤ ✤ ✤ ✤

Come, O true light!
Come, O powerful one,
who always creates and recreates
and transforms by Your will alone!
Come, O eternal joy!
Come, You who alone go to the lonely,
for as You see I am lonely!
Come, O breath and life!
Come, O my joy, my glory and my endless delight!
I thank You
that You have become one spirit with me,
without confusion, without mutation,
without transformation,
You, the God of all,
and that You have become everything for me.

I give You thanks that for me
You have become light that does not set and glory

that does not decline.
and have nowhere to hide Yourself.
No, You have never hidden Yourself from anyone,
but we are the ones who always hide from You,
by refusing to go to You;
but then, where would You hide,
You who find nowhere a place of repose?

ST. SYMEON THE NEW THEOLOGIAN

The Angelic Salutation

Hail! Mary, full of grace, the Lord is with You. O Virgin Theotokos: Blessed are you among women, and blessed is the fruit of your womb, for you have given the Savior of our souls.

A Prayer Request to Your Patron Saint

Pray to God for me O Holy Saint _____, for You are well-pleasing to God. I entreat you to help me by interceding to God for my soul.

A Prayer Request to Your Guardian Angel

O Holy Angel,
Guardian and protector of my soul and body,
Heavenly companion of my life,
Do not abandon me, a sinner,
Nor let the enemy overwhelm
    me through my weaknesses.
Take hold of my weak and feeble
    hand and guide me on the
    way of salvation.
Yes, O Holy Angel of God, guardian
    and protector of my soul and body,
Overlook the many ways by which
    I have grieved you,
All the days of my life.
Protect me during this day,
And guard me from every
    temptation of the evil one,
That I may not anger God by
    falling into sin.
Pray for me that I may have
    a holy fear of not offending God,
And that I may prove to be a
    worthy servant of His goodness.   AMEN.

The Hymn to the Theotokos

It is truly meet to bless you, O Theotokos, ever-blessed and most pure, and the Mother of our God. More honorable than the Cherubim, and more glorious beyond compare than the Seraphim: without defilement you gave birth to God the Word: true Theotokos, we magnify you.

Prayer on Entering Church

I rejoiced when they said to me:
Let us go into the house of the Lord.
I come into your house with thanksgiving
    and praise, O Lord.
Lead me, O Lord, in the paths of Your righteousness,
Make Your way straight before me
That with a pure heart and a clean mind
I may glorify You, forever,
One Godhead worshiped in Three Persons:
Father, Son and Holy Spirit. Amen.

Prayer Upon Leaving Church

Lord, now let your servant depart in peace,
According to Your Word:
For my eyes have seen Your salvation,
Which You have prepared
Before the face of all people;
A light to provide light for the Gentiles,
And the glory of Your people Israel.

Prayer Before the Icon of Christ

We reverence Your spotless icon, O gracious Lord, and ask forgiveness of our transgressions, O Christ our God: for of Your own good will You were pleased to be nailed to the Cross in the flesh, that You might deliver from bondage to the enemy those whom You had fashioned. Wherefore, we cry out to You with praise: You have filled all things with joy, O Savior, for You came to save the world.

Prayer to Christ the True Light

Christ our God, the True Light
Who enlightens and sanctifies every person
    who comes into the world:
Seal us with the Light of Your Countenance
    that we may perceive Thy
    Unapproachable Radiance.
Direct the footsteps of our life in the way
    of Your commandments.
Through the prayers of Your all-pure Mother
    and of all Your saints. AMEN.

Prayer Before the Icon of the Theotokos

Because you are a well-spring
    of tenderness, O Theotokos,
Make us worthy of compassion.
Look upon us, a sinful people.
Manifest your power as always,
For, hoping in you, we shout with joy:
Hail! as once did the Angel Gabriel,
Chief of the Bodiless Powers.

A Prayer Before Undertaking Any Task

Almighty God, our help and refuge,
Source of all wisdom and
Pillar of strength,
You know that without You I am powerless.
I firmly believe that "apart from You I can
   do nothing."
Send Your grace to enable me to complete
   the task I am about to undertake.
Help me to accomplish it faithfully and diligently
So that it may prove helpful to myself and others.
And that it may bring glory to Your holy Name.
For Yours is the kingdom and the power
   and the glory of the Father and
   the Son and the Holy Spirit now
   and forevermore. AMEN.

Prayer Upon Completion of a Task

Thank You, Lord, for the strength and guidance
   You gave me to help me complete my task.
Without Your help, I could not have done it.
Thank You for being the fulfillment of all good things.
Fill my soul so that it may overflow with Your joy and

gladness.
And save me, for You are all-merciful. Amen.

Prayer for One Who is Suffering

Lord, how inscrutable are Your ways.
We confess that our thoughts are not Your thoughts.
And our ways are not Your ways.
You love us far more than we love You,
And Your wisdom is far superior to ours.
Help us to yield our will to Yours,
And our puny knowledge to Your Grand Wisdom.
Help us to see Your love behind everything
     that happens to us.
For You are at work for good in our lives
     when we place our complete trust in You.
You know, Lord, how confused our minds are,
     And what great distress afflicts our hearts.
In our utter weakness we cry out to You,
     "My God, my God, why have You forsaken us?"
Have mercy, Lord, have mercy on us.
Relieve the pain of (name) who is a victim of so
     much senseless suffering and pain.
Do not prolong his/her agony.
We confess that You are never
     Nearer to us than when our

hearts are broken.
Come to us in our weakness, Lord,
    Increase our faith.
Help us to pray as You did in Your agony,
    "Shall I not drink the cup which You,
    the Father has given me?"
You are our only hope, dear Lord,
    we seek refuge under the shelter of Your wings.
We bow down before You, the God of
    mercies and bounties.
Full of love for Your children.
    You alone are the Physician of our souls
    and bodies,
And to You we give glory, to the Father,
    And to the Son, and to the Holy Spirit now and
forever. AMEN.

Prayers from the Bible

A Prayer of Trust
(Psalm 131)
My heart is not proud, O Lord,
my eyes are not haughty;
I do not concern myself with great matters
or things too wonderful for me.
But I have stilled and quieted my soul;
like a weaned child with its mother,
like a weaned child is my soul within me.

O Israel, put your hope in the Lord
both now and for evermore.

Psalm of Thanksgiving

I give You thanks, O Lord, with my
            whole heart;
    before the angels I sing Your praise;
I bow before Your holy presence
    and give thanks to Your name for
    Your steadfast love and Your faithfulness;
For You have exalted above everything
    Your name and Your word.
On the day I called, You answered me;
    my strength of soul You increased.
Though I walk in the midst of trouble,
    You preserve my life;
You stretch out Your hand against the wrath
    of my adversaries,
    and your right hand delivers me.
The Lord will fulfill His purpose for me;
    Your steadfast love, O Lord, endures forever.

PSALM 138:1-3,7-8

Paul's Prayer for the Corinthians

(II Corinthians 1:3-5)
Praise be to the God and Father of our Lord Jesus
Christ, the Father of compassion and the God of all
comfort, who comforts us in all our troubles, so that
we can comfort those in any trouble with the comfort

we ourselves have received from God. For just as the sufferings of Christ flow over into our lives, so also through Christ our comfort overflows.

Prayer for the Coming of Jesus
(Revelation 22:20b)
Amen. Come, Lord Jesus.

Praise for Creation
(Psalm 8)
O Lord, our Lord,
how majestic is Your name
in all the earth!
You have set your glory
above the heavens.
From the lips of children and infants
You have ordained praise
because of Your enemies,
to silence the foe and the avenger.
When I consider Your heavens,
the work of Your fingers,
the moon and the stars,
which You have set in place,
what is man that You are mindful of him,
the son of man that You care for him?
You made him a little lower than
the heavenly beings
and crowned him with glory and honour.
You made him ruler over the works

of Your hands;
You put everything under his feet:
all flocks and herds,
and the beasts of the field,
the birds of the air
and the fish of the sea,
all that swim the paths of the seas.
O Lord, our Lord,
how majestic is Your name
in all the earth!

The Publican's Prayer
(Luke 18:13)
God be merciful to me the sinner. (KJV)

The Dying Thief's Prayer
(Luke 23:42)
"Jesus, remember me when You come into your kingdom."

Stephen's Dying Prayer
(Acts 7:60a)
"Lord, do not hold this sin against them."

Paul's Conversion Prayer
(Acts 22:10)
"What shall I do, Lord?"

Paul's Prayer for the Church at Ephesus
(Ephesians 3:14-21)

For this reason I kneel before the Father, from whom His whole family in heaven and on earth derives its name. I pray that out of His glorious riches He may strengthen you with power through His Spirit in your inner being, so that Christ may dwell in your hearts through faith. And I pray that you, being rooted and established in love, may have power, together with all the saints, to grasp how wide and long and high and deep is the love of Christ, and to know this love that surpasses knowledge–that you may be filled to the measure of all the fullness of God.

Now to Him who is able to do immeasurably more than all we ask or imagine, according to His power that is at work within us, to Him be glory in the church and in Christ Jesus throughout all generations, for ever and ever! Amen.

Mary's Song of Praise
(Luke 1:46-55)

My soul praises the Lord
and my spirit rejoices in God my Savior,
for He has been mindful of the humble state of His servant.
From now on all generations will call me blessed,
for the Mighty One has done great things for me–
holy is His name.
His mercy extends to those who fear Him,

from generation to generation.
He has performed mighty deeds with His arm;
He has scattered those who are proud in their inmost
thoughts.
He has brought down rulers from their thrones
but has lifted up the humble.
He has filled the hungry with good things
but has sent the rich away empty.
He has helped His servant Israel,
remembering to be merciful
to Abraham and His descendants for ever,
even as He said to our fathers.

Jesus' Prayer for Deliverance
(Mark 14:36)
Abba, Father, everything is possible for You. Take this
cup from me. Yet not what I will, but what You will.

Paul's Prayer for the Ephesians
Ephesians 3:14-19
I kneel before the Father, from whom the whole family in heaven and on earth derives its name. I pray that out of His glorious riches He may strengthen you with power though His Spirit in your inner being, so that Christ may dwell in your hearts through faith. And I pray that you, being rooted and established in love, may have power, together with all the saints, to grasp how wide and long and high and deep is the love of Christ, and to know this love that surpasses knowl-

edge–that you may be filled to the measure of all the fullness of God.

The High Priestly Prayer of Jesus
(John 17:1-9)

"Father, the time has come. Glorify your Son, that Your Son may glorify You. For You granted Him authority over all people that He might give eternal life to all those You have given Him. Now this is eternal life: that they may know You, the only true God, and Jesus Christ, whom You have sent. I have brought You glory on earth by completing the work You gave Me to do. And now, Father, glorify Me in Your presence with the glory I had with You before the world began.

"I have revealed You to those whom You gave Me out of the world. They were Yours; You gave them to me and they obeyed Your word. Now they know that everything You have given Me comes from You. For I gave them the words You gave me and they accepted them. They knew with certainty that I came from You, and they believed that You sent me. I pray for them. I am not praying for the world, but for those You have given me, for they are Yours. All I have is Yours, and all You have is mine. And glory has come to Me through them. I will remain in the world no longer, but they are still in the world, and I am coming to You. Holy Father, protect them by the power of Your name–the name You gave Me–so that they may be one as We are one. While I was with them, I protected them and kept them safe by that name You gave Me. None has been lost except the One doomed to destruction so that Scripture would be fulfilled.

"I am coming to You now, but I say these things while I am still in the world, so that they may have the full measure of My joy within them. I have given them Your word and the world has hated them, for they are not of the world any more than I am of the world. My prayer is not that You take them out of the world but that You protect them from the evil one. They are not of the world, even as I am not of it. Sanctify them by the Truth; Your word is Truth. As You sent Me into the world, I have sent them into the world. For them I sanctify Myself, that they too may be truly sanctified."

Jesus Prays at Gethsemane
(Matthew 26:39)
"My Father, if it is possible, may this cup be taken from Me. Yet not as I will, but as You will."

A Prayer From the Cross
(Luke 23:34, 43, 46)
"Father, forgive them; for they know not what they do....Verily I say unto thee, Today shalt thou be with me in paradise....Father, into Your hands I commend My spirit." (KJV)

Matthew 27:46

"Eli, Eli, la-ma sa-bach-that-ni? that is to say, My God, my God, why hast Thou forsaken Me?" (KJV)

A Prayer for Refuge
(Psalm 31:1-5)
In You, O Lord, I have taken refuge;
    let me never be put to shame;
    deliver me in Your righteousness.
Turn your ear to me,
    come quickly to my rescue;
be my rock of refuge,
    a strong fortress to save me.
Since You are my rock and my fortress,
    for the sake of Your name lead and guide me.
Free me from the trap that is set for me,
    for You are my refuge.
Into Your hands I commit my spirit;
    redeem me, O Lord, the God of truth.

A Prayer of Praise
(Psalm 9:1-2)
I will praise You, O Lord, with all my heart;
    I will tell of all Your wonders.
I will be glad and rejoice in You;
    I will sing praise to Your name, O Most High.

The Prayer of Jesus at the Raising of Lazarus
(John 11:41b-42)
"Father, I thank You that You have heard Me. I knew that You always hear Me, but I said this for the benefit of the people standing here, that they may believe that You sent Me."

Thanks for Comfort
(Psalm 23:4-5)
Yea, though I walk through the valley of the shadow of death, I will fear no evil for Thou art with me; Thy rod and Thy staff they comfort me.

Thou preparest a table before me in the presence of mine enemies, Thou anointest my head with oil; my cup runneth over (KJV).

Prayers Before Communion

O Lord, I am not worthy that Thou shouldest come under my roof, but relying on Thy lovingkindness I draw near to Thine Altar:
A sick man, to the Physician of life:
A blind man, to the Light of eternal brightness;
Poor, to the Lord of heaven and earth;
Naked, to the King of Glory;
A sheep, to its Shepherd;
A creature, to its Creator;
Desolate, to the living Comforter;
Miserable, to the Merciful;

A Sinner, to the Giver of pardon;
Ungodly, to the Justifier;
Beseeching Your exuberant and infinite mercy that it
may please Thee–

> To heal my weakness,
> To enlighten my blindness,
> To enrich my poverty,
> To clothe my nakedness,
> To bring me back from wanderings,
> To console my desolation,
> To reconcile my guiltiness,
> To give pardon to the sinner,
> > forgiveness to the miserable,
> > life to the lost,
> > justification to the dead;
> > so that I may be enabled to receive Thee,
> > The Bread of Life
> > The King of Kings, and
> > Lord of Lords. AMEN

✠ ✠ ✠ ✠ ✠

You have taken me captive with longing for You, O
Christ,
And have transformed me with Your divine love.
Burn up my sins with the fire of Your Spirit
And count me worthy to take my fill of delight in You
So that, dancing with joy, I may magnify Your two
comings.

Prayer of St. Symeon the Translator

O only pure and sinless Lord, Who through the ineffable compassion of Your love for us did assume our whole nature through the pure and virgin blood of her who supernaturally conceived You by the coming of the Divine Spirit and by the will of the Eternal Father; O Christ Jesus, Wisdom and Peace and Power of God, Who in Your assumption of our nature did suffer Your life-giving and saving Passion–the Cross, the Nails, the Spear and Death–mortify all the deadly passions of my body. You Who in Your burial did spoil the dominions of hell, bury with good thoughts my evil schemes and scatter the spirits of wickedness. You Who by Your life-giving Resurrection on the third day did raise up our fallen first Parent, raise me up who am sunk in sin and suggest to me ways of repentance. You Who by Your glorious Ascension did deify our nature which You had assumed and did honor it by Your session at the right hand of the Father, make me worthy by partaking of Your holy Mysteries of a place at Your right hand among those who are saved. You Who by the descent of the Spirit, the Paraclete, did make Your holy Disciples worthy vessels, make me also a recipient of His coming. You Who art to come again to judge the world with justice, grant me also to meet You on the clouds, my Maker and Creator, with all Your Saints, that I may unendingly glorify and praise You with Your Eternal Father and Thy all-holy and good and life-giving Spirit, now and ever, and to the ages of ages. Amen.

First Prayer of St. John Damascene

O sovereign Lord Jesus Christ our God, Who alone has authority to forgive us our sins, overlook in Your goodness and love for us all my offenses whether committed with knowledge or in ignorance, and make me worthy to receive without condemnation Your divine, glorious, spotless, and life-giving Mysteries, not for punishment, nor for an increase of sins, but for purification and sanctification and as a pledge of the life and kingdom to come, as a protection and help, and for the destruction of enemies, and for the blotting out of my many transgressions. For You are a God of mercy and compassion and love for us, and to You we send up the glory, with the Father and the Holy Spirit, now and ever, and to the ages of ages. AMEN.

Second Prayer of St. Basil the Great

I know, O Lord, that I partake of Your immaculate Body and precious Blood unworthily, and that I am guilty, and eat and drink judgment to myself by not discerning the Body and blood of You my Christ and God. But taking courage from your compassion I approach You, for You have said: "He who eats My Flesh and drinks My Blood abides in Me and I in him." Therefore have compassion O Lord, and do not make an example of me, a sinner, but deal with me according to Your mercy; and let these Holy Things be for my healing and purification and enlightenment and protection and salvation and sanctification of body and soul, for the turning away of every fantasy and all evil practice and diabolical activity working subconsciously in my members, for confidence and love towards You, for reformation of life and security, for an increase of virtue and perfection, for fulfillment of the commandments, for communion with the Holy Spirit, as a provision for eternal life, and as an acceptable defense at Your dread Tribunal, not for judgment or for condemnation.

Fourth Prayer of St. John Chrysostom

I believe, O Lord, and I confess that You are truly the Christ, the Son of the Living God, Who came into the world to save sinners, of whom I am the chief. And I believe that this is Your pure Body and Your own precious Blood. Therefore, I pray to You, have mercy on me and forgive my transgressions, voluntary and involuntary, in word and deed, known and unknown. And grant that I may partake of Your Holy Mysteries without condemnation, for the remission of sins and for life eternal. AMEN.

Prayers of St. Symeon the Translator

Behold I approach for Divine Communion. O Creator, let me not be burnt by communicating, for You are Fire which burns the unworthy. But purify me from every stain.

Of your Mystical Supper, O Son of God, accept me today as a communicant; for I will not speak of the Mystery to Your enemies; I will not give You a kiss like Judas, but like the Thief do I confess You. Remember me, O Lord, in Your Kingdom.

Tremble, O man, when you see the deifying Blood, for it is a coal that burns the unworthy. The Body of God both deifies and nourishes; it deifies the spirit and wondrously nourishes the mind.

You have ravished me with longing, O Christ, and with Your divine love You have changed me.
But burn up with spiritual fire my sins and make me worthy to be filled with delight in You, that I may leap for joy, O gracious Lord, and magnify Your two comings.

Into the splendor of Your Saints how shall I who am unworthy enter? For if I dare to enter the bridechamber, my vesture betrays me, for it is not a wedding garment, and as a prisoner I shall be cast out by the Angels. Cleanse my soul from the pollution of sin and save me, O Lord, in Your love for mankind.

Sovereign Lover of humankind, Lord Jesus my God, let not these Holy Gifts be to me for judgment through my being unworthy, but for purification and sanctification of my soul and body, and as a pledge of the life and kingdom to come. For it is good for me to cling to God and to place in the Lord my hope and salvation.

Prayers After Communion

Prayer of St. Basil the Great

Lord Christ our God, King of the ages and Creator of all, I thank You for the blessings You have granted me and for the communion of Your pure and life-giving Mysteries. I pray You, therefore, gracious Lord and Lover of mankind, guard me under Your protection and within the shadow of Your wings; and grant me with a clear conscience till my last breath worthily to partake of Your sacred Gifts for forgiveness of sins and for life eternal. For You are the Bread of Life, the Source of Holiness, the Giver of all that is good, and to You we send up the glory, with the Father and the Holy Spirit, now and ever and to the ages of ages. AMEN.

Prayer of St. Symeon the Translator

O You Who give me willingly Your Flesh for food, You Who are fire, and burn the unworthy, scorch me not, O my Maker, but rather pass through me for the integration of my members, into all my joints, my affections, and my heart. Burn up the thorns of all my sins. Purify my soul, sanctify my mind; strengthen my knees and bones; Enlighten the simplicity of my five senses. Nail down the whole of me with Your fear. Ever protect, guard, and keep me from every soul-destroying word and act. Sanctify, purify, attune, and rule me. Adorn me, give me understanding, and enlighten me. Make me the temple of Your Spirit alone, and no longer a habitation of sin: that having become Your house by receiving Holy Communion, every evil spirit and passion may flee from me like fire. I bring to You as intercessors all the saints, the ranks of the Heavenly Hosts, Your Forerunner, the wise Apostles, and Your pure and immaculate Mother. Receive their prayers, my compassionate Christ. And make Your slave a child of light. For You alone art our salvation, O Good One, and the radiance of our souls, and to You as our Lord and God as is right we all give glory day and night.

Prayers of Thanksgiving

I thank Thee, O Lord my God, for that Thou hast not rejected me, a sinner, but hast suffered me to be a partaker of Thy holy gifts. I thank Thee that unworthy as I am Thou hast enabled me to receive of Thy most pure and heavenly gifts. And yet moreover I beseech Thee, O Lord and lover of mankind, who for our sakes didst die and rise again, and hast provided us these dread and life-giving mysteries unto the benefit and hallowing of our souls and bodies: Grant that these Thy gifts may be even unto me for the healing of soul and body, and the driving out of every adversary; for the enlightening of the eyes of my understanding, and peace for the powers of my soul; for faith unashamed, and love without dissimulation; for the fullness of wisdom, and the keeping of Thy commandments; for the increase of Thy divine grace, and an inheritance in Thy kingdom. That preserved by them in Thy holiness I may be ever mindful of Thy grace, and not henceforth live unto myself but unto Thee, our bountiful Lord.

And when I have departed this life in the hope of life everlasting, vouchsafe that I may enter into eternal rest, where the voice of them that flourish is unceasing, and the delight of them that behold the unsearchable beauty of Thy countenance knoweth no bound: For Thou art the true desire and the ineffable joy of them that love Thee, O Christ our God, and all creation doth sing Thy praise, for ever and ever. Amen.

Another Prayer

Lord Jesus Christ our God, may Thy sacred body be for me unto life everlasting, and Thy precious blood unto remission of sins. May this Eucharist be for me unto joy, health and gladness. And at Thy dread second coming, account me, a sinner, worthy to stand on the right hand of Thy glory: By the prayers of Thy most holy Mother, and of all the saints.

Intercessory Prayer to the Mother of God

Most holy Mother of God, who art the light of my darkened soul; my hope, my refuge and shelter; my comfort and my joy: I give thee thanks for that thou hast suffered me, unworthy as I am to be a partaker of the pure body and precious blood of thy Son. Do Thou who didst bring forth the true light, enlighten the eyes of my understanding. Thou that gavest birth to the fountain of immortality, quicken me who am slain by sin. Thou who art all compassion, O Mother of the merciful God, have mercy upon me, and bestow on me the spirit of remorse and a contrite heart. Give me lowliness of mind. Loose my captive thoughts. And vouchsafe that even unto my last breath I may without condemnation receive the hallowing of the most pure sacrament unto the healing of soul and body. And grant me the grace of repentance and confession that I may praise and glorify thee all the days of my life. For blessed art thou and all glorious for ever and ever. AMEN.

The Song of Simeon

Lord, now lettest Thou thy servant depart in peace, according to Thy word:

> For mine eyes have seen Thy salvation,
> Which Thou hast prepared before the face of
> all people;
> A light to lighten the Gentiles, and the
> glory of Thy people Israel.

✠ ✠ ✠ ✠ ✠

Blessed are those who have eaten
          from the bread of love which is Jesus.
This is the wine that gladdens human hearts.
This is the wine which the lustful have drunk
          and they have become chaste,
the sinners and they forgot the ways of
          unrighteousness,
the drunkards and they became fasters,
the rich and they became desirous of poverty,
the poor and they became rich in hope,
the sick and they became courageous,
the fools and they became wise.

MYSTICAL TREATISES, ST. ISAAC THE SYRIAN, 7TH CENTURY

Holy Week Prayers

Saint Tikhon Zadonsky on the Crucifixion

You lived on earth, King of Heaven, to lead me to
heaven–I who had been cast out of paradise.
You were born in the flesh of the Virgin to give me
birth in the spirit.
You suffered insults
to silence the mouths of my enemies
who denounced me.
You abased Yourself, You Who are higher than all
honors, in order to honor me, the dishonored.

You wept to wipe the tears from my eyes.
You sighed, grieved, sorrowed to save me from sighing, grieving, suffering pain through eternity, to give me eternal joy and gladness.
You were sold and betrayed
that I might be freed, I who was enslaved.
You were bound that my bonds might be broken.
You were submitted to an unjust trial–
You Who are the Judge of all the earth–
that I might be freed from eternal judgement.
You were made naked in order to clothe me in the robes of salvation, in the garments of gladness.
You were crowned with thorns,
that I might receive the crown of life.
You were called the king in mockery–You, the King of all!–to open the kingdom of heaven for me.
Your head was lashed with a reed
that my name should be written in the book of life.
You suffered outside the city gates in order to
lead me, one who had been cast out of paradise.
into the eternal Jerusalem.
You were put among evil men–You Who are the only Just One–that I, the unjust, might be justified.
You were cursed, the One Blessed,
that I, the accursed, should be blessed.
You shed Your blood that my sins might be
cleansed away.
You were given vinegar to drink
that I might eat and drink at the feast in

Your Kingdom.
You died, You Who are the life of all–
in order to revive me, the dead.
You were laid in the tomb
that I might rise from the tomb.
You were brought to life again
that I might believe in my resurrection.

Good Friday Prayer

Each part of your body suffered some outrage
because of us:

Your head, the thorns:
Your face, spitting;
Your mouth; the taste of vinegar and gall;
Your ears, injurious blasphemies;
Your shoulders, the purple derision;
Your back, flagellation;
Your hand, the reed;
Your entire body, the pangs of the cross;
Your members, the nails;
Your side, the lance.
You who have suffered for us, and who in suffering
have freed us,
You who, through love of man, have lowered Yourself
with us and who have lifted us up, Savior, have mercy
on us (GOOD FRIDAY HYMN).

Paschal Prayers

Christ is risen from the dead. By His death He has destroyed death. And to those in the tombs He has bestowed life.

Having Beheld the Resurrection

Having beheld the resurrection of Christ,
Let us worship the holy Lord Jesus, the only
sinless One.
We venerate Thy Cross, O Christ
And we praise and glorify Thy holy resurrection;
for Thou art our God and we know no other
than Thee.
We call on Thy name,
O Come all ye faithful,
Let us venerate Christ's holy resurrection!
For behold, through the cross joy has come
into all the world.
Let us ever bless the Lord, praising His resurrection,
For by enduring the cross for us,
He has destroyed death by death.

–FROM THE MATINS SERVICE

The Pascha of the Lord

The Pascha (passover) of the Lord,
From death unto life,
And from earth unto heaven
Has Christ our God brought us over....

Now are all things filled with light,
Heaven and earth and the places under the earth.
All Creation does celebrate the Resurrection
of Christ.
On whom it is founded....
We celebrate the death of Death,
The annihilation of Hell,
The beginning of a new life and everlasting.
And with ecstasy we sing praises to the author there-
of....

This is the chosen and holy Day,
The one King and Lord of Sabbaths,
The Feast of Feasts and the Triumph of Triumphs....

O Christ, the Passover, great and most holy!
O Wisdom, Word and Power of God!
Grant that we may more perfectly partake of Thee
In the day of Thy Kingdom which knoweth no night.

–FROM THE ORTHODOX EASTER MATINS

Your Death, O Lord, Became the Cause of Immortality

Your death, O Lord, became the cause of immortality, for if You had not been placed in a tomb, paradise
would not have been opened.

We celebrate the death of Death, the downfall of
Hell, and the beginning of a life new and everlasting.
Glory to Thy holy resurrection, O Christ.

Today Hell Groans

Today hell groans and cries aloud, "My dominion has been swallowed up; the Shepherd has been crucified and He has raised Adam. I am deprived of those whom I once ruled; in my strength I devoured them, but now I have cast them forth. He who was crucified has emptied the tombs, the power of death has no more strength. "Glory to Thy Cross, O Lord, and to Thy Resurrection."

–THE PASCHAL VIGIL

What shall we give in return to the Lord for his gifts?
For us he became human
    and on account of our corrupted nature
    the Word became flesh and dwelt in our midst.
He was the benefactor to those who were ungrateful,
the liberator to those in bondage
and the sun of righteousness to those who
dwell in darkness.
He who was incorrupt
ascended on the cross,
the light descended into hades,
the life suffered death,
and he was the resurrection for those who had fallen.
Let us sing to him: Our God, glory to you!

RESURRECTION MATINS HYMN

Hades Was Overcome

Hades was overcome. The gatekeepers threw away their keys and fled as they saw Christ crush and break the bolts of the door....Suddenly the bodies of the dead became animated. They were resurrected, and they trampled upon Hades, crying out, 'O unjust one, where is thy victory, and Death, where is thy sting?' Suddenly all of the tombs were opened of themselves, and all of the dead were released from them and formed a chorus...In return for these things, O Redeemer, what do we have to offer except a doxology? Therefore, spare, O Christ our God, those who believe in Thy cross, tomb and resurrection. Grant to us forgiveness of sins. And whenever the "awakening" common to all comes, consider us worthy to see Thy face and to hear Thy voice with confidence."

(ON THE RESURRECTION IV-ST. ROMANOS THE MELODIST)

Led Away as a Lamb

For this one
Who was led away as a lamb,
and who was sacrificed as a
sheep.
By Himself delivered us from
servitude to the world,
as from the land of Egypt,
and released us from bondage
to the devil
as from the hand of Pharaoh,

and sealed our souls by his
own spirit
and the members of our bodies
by his own blood.
This is the one who delivered
us
from slavery into freedom,
from darkness into light,
from death into life,
from tyranny into an eternal
kingdom,
and who made us a new
priesthood,
and a special people forever.
Glory to Thy holy resurrection, O Lord.

- MELITO OF SARDIS, SECOND CENTURY

Yesterday I Was Crucified With Him

Yesterday I was crucified with Him;
today I am glorified with Him.
Yesterday I died with Him;
today I am made alive in Him.
Yesterday, I was buried with Him,
today I am raised up with Him.
Let us offer ourselves to Him
who suffered and rose again for us.
Let us become divine for His sake,
since for us He became human.
He assumed the worse that He might give

us the better.

He became poor that by His poverty we might
become rich.

He accepted the form of a servant
that we might win back our freedom.

He came down that we might be lifted up.

He was tempted that through Him we might conquer.

He was dishonoured that He might glorify us.

He died that He might save us.

He ascended that He might draw to Himself us,
who were thrown down through the fall of sin.

Let us give all, offer all, to Him
Who gave Himself a ransom and reconciliation for us.

We needed an incarnate God, a God put to death,
that we might live.

We were put to death together with Him
that we might be cleansed.

We rose again with Him
because we were put to death with Him.

We were glorified with Him
because we rose again with Him.

A few drops of blood
recreate the whole creation!

EASTER ORATION, ST. GREGORY THE THEOLOGIAN, 4TH CENTURY

Preparing for Holy Confession
An Examination of Conscience*

To help you personally prepare for the Sacrament of Confession we suggest you find time to sit quietly, and to prayerfully examine your life using as a guide the following examination of conscience.

1. *When Jesus saw him there and learned that he had been in this condition for a long time, he asked him, "Do you want to get well?"* (JOHN 5:6).

What is my attitude to this confession? Have I prepared for it? Am I sincerely willing to change aspects of my life so that they will be more in keeping with the Gospel? Did I forget or hide any serious sins in my last confession? Have I made reparation to anyone I have injured? Since my last confession have I remained firm in my efforts to change my life, or did I give up due to laziness, discouragement or forgetfulness?

2. *Jesus said: "Love the Lord your God with all your heart and with all your soul and with all your mind. This is the first and greatest commandment"* (MATTHEW 22:37-8).

---

* This "Examination" is from the booklet, "Preparing for Confession" by L. Joseph Letendre published by Light & Life Publishing Company.

Do I really love God above all things? Or are worldly things such as possessions, power or popularity more important to me? Have I placed my trust in these or in such things as horoscopes, occult practices and superstitions?

Have I prayed on a regular and daily basis? Do I pray attentively? Do I approach prayer with joy and enthusiasm, or do I allow anything, no matter how trivial, to be an excuse to shorten prayer or avoid it entirely? Do I think about God during the course of my day?

3. *Jesus said, "Whoever acknowledges me before men, I will also acknowledge before my Father in heaven. But whoever disowns me before men, I will disown him before my Father in heaven"* (MATTHEW 10:32-3).

Am I willing to be known as a Christian in public and private life? Was I embarrassed or afraid to admit my belief in Christ and His Church to others? If someone said something unfair or inaccurate about Christ or Christianity, did I try to speak the truth with gentleness, respect and love?

4. *Always be prepared to give an answer to everyone who asks you to give the reason for the hope that you have* (I PETER 3:15).

Do I know what the Orthodox Church teaches and believes? Did I take the time to read, study, or learn more about my faith? Am I able and willing to answer questions about Christ, the Church and my faith?

Do I read, study or meditate on God's Word in the Bible daily?

5. *Ascribe to the LORD the glory due his name. Bring an offering and come before him; worship the LORD in the splendor of his holiness*

(I CHRONICLES 16:29)

Do I keep Sundays and feast days holy by participating as fully as possible in the liturgical services? Do I observe the fasting days and seasons of the Church? Do I receive our Lord's Body and Blood in Holy Communion by prayer and fasting?

6. *Submit yourselves to one another out of reverence for Christ* (EPHESIANS 5:21)

Have I honored and obeyed my parents, showing them love and respect and helping them with their material, emotional and spiritual needs? Have I been loving, patient and understanding with my children? Did I discipline them appropriately? Have I tried to impart my faith to them by word and example? Do I contribute to the peace and well-being of my family by offering my time, service and love?

In my job or profession, am I an honest and hard worker? Do I view the service I render my employers and others as service done to and for Christ? Do I pay my employees a just wage? Are my expectations of them fair and reasonable? Have I fulfilled my promises, contracts and obligations?

Have I respected and obeyed legitimate authority? Have I voted responsibly and knowledgeably? Have I paid my taxes? Do I work, as I am able, to promote peace, justice, morality and love in my community, my country, and the world?

Do I use my positions of responsibility and authority for the good of others?

7. *Jesus said: "Love your enemies. Do good to those who hate you, bless those who curse you, pray for those who mistreat you. If anyone strikes you on one cheek, turn to him the other also. If someone takes your cloak, do not stop him from taking your tunic"* (LUKE 6:27-9).

Have I caused injury to another's life, health, spiritual or emotional well-being, or material possessions by violence or neglect?
Have I advised or helped in the obtaining of an abortion?

Have I quarreled, been unduly angry with or insulted anyone? Have I been reconciled with them? If I have injured or offended anyone, have I sought their forgiveness? If anyone has injured or offended me, have I forgiven them? Or am I still filled with hatred and a desire for revenge?

Am I committed to accepting suffering rather than inflicting it?

Did I seek to retaliate in the face of provocation and violence of any sort?

Do I strive for peace within myself and work to be a peacemaker in my daily life?

8. *It is God's will that you should be holy; that you should avoid sexual immorality; that each of you should learn to control his own body in a way that is holy and honorable, not in passionate lust like the heathen, who do not know God*

(I THESSALONIANS 4:5-6).

Have I been faithful to my spouse?

Have I exercised self-control in regards to food, drink, drugs, and sexual desire? Have misused my sexuality for fornication, masturbation, impure thoughts and fantasies? Have I participated in indecent conversations or made use of pornographic entertainment, pictures or reading?

Have I encouraged others to sin by my own failures in this area?

9. *Jesus said, "Be on your guard against all kinds of greed; a man's life does not consist in the abundance of his possessions"* (LUKE 12:15).

Have I envied or desired inordinately another's position or property? Have I stolen or damaged the property of others? Did I restore it or make restitution?

Do I share my possessions with those who have less? Do I give freely and generously of my time, talent and money to those in need and/or the church?

10. *If anyone considers himself religious and yet does not keep a tight rein on his tongue, he deceives himself and his religion is worthless* (JAMES 1:26).

Have I taken the name of the Lord in vain? Have I blasphemed or used profane language?

Do I talk too much or listen too little?

Have I lied or, by cowardly silence, have I avoided telling the truth? Have I gossiped or spread rumors about others? Have I spoken harshly, unjustly, unnecessarily or insultingly to anyone about anyone?

Do I spend time in silence? Or must I always be talking or having the radio or television on?

Have I been boastful about myself or judgmental about others?

11. *Whatever you do, do it all for the glory of God*
                                        (I CORINTHIANS 10:31).

Is all that I do motivated first and foremost by a desire to love and serve God and my neighbor in the way that God wills me to?

Do I think of myself as better than others?

When I pray, fast or do any good, do I try to do it secretly? Or, by word or display, do I make sure that others notice me and my works?

12. *Cast your cares on the LORD and he will sustain you; he will never let the righteous fall* (PSALM 55:22).

Am I anxious or worried about anything? Is there a problem or hurt that I should bring to the Lord in Confession for forgiveness, healing or guidance?

St. John Chrysostom on Repentance

"No sin is so great it can conquer the munificence of the Master. Even if one is a fornicator, or an adulterer...the power of the gift and the love of the Master are great enough to make all these sins disappear and to make the sinner shine more brightly than the rays of the sun..."

"And Christ Himself, addressing the whole human race, said: "Come to me, all you who labor and are burdened, and I will give you rest....""

"His invitation is one of kindness, His goodness is beyond description....""

"And see whom He calls! Those who have spent their strength in breaking the law, those who are burdened with their sins, those who can no longer lift up their heads, those who are filled with shame, those who can no longer speak out. And why does He call them? Not to demand an account, not to hold court. But why? To relieve them of their pain, to take away their heavy burden. For what could ever be a heavier burden than sin?....I shall refresh you who are weighted down by sin, He says, and you who are bent down as if under a burden; I shall grant you remission of your sins. Only come to Me!"

Two Church Fathers on Repentance

"Repentance (metanoia) is fitting at all times and for all persons, for sinners as well as for the righteous who look for salvation. There are no bounds to perfection, for even the perfection of the most perfect is nothing but imperfection. Hence, until the moment of death, neither the time nor the works of perfection can ever be complete" (St. Isaac of Syria).

"Do all in your power not to fall, for the strong athlete should not fall. But if you do fall, get up again at once and continue the contest. Even if you fall a thousand times...rise up again each time, and keep on doing this until the day of your death. For it is written, 'If a righteous man falls seven times' – that is repeatedly throughout his life–seven times 'shall he rise again'" (St. John of Karpathos).

St. John Climacus

How well these words by St. John Climacus reflect God's mercy:

"It is the property of angels not to fall, and even, as some say, it is quite impossible for them to fall. It is the property of men to fall, and to rise again as often as this may happen. But it is the property of devils, and devils alone, not to rise once they have fallen."

Prayers of Confession

Prayer of Manasses (King of Juda)

O Lord Almighty, God of our fathers Abraham and Isaac and Jacob and of their righteous descendants, who made heaven and earth with all their adornment, who encompassed the sea with the word of Your command, who closed the deep and sealed it with Your fearful and glorious name, whose presence all things revere and before whose power they quake, because the magnificence of Your glory is unendurable, and irresistible the wrath of Your threat against sinners; the kindness of Your promise is both immeasurable, and inscrutable, for You are the Lord most high, compassionate, long-suffering and most merciful, offering atonement for the evils of men.

You, O Lord, in the abundance of Your goodness, promised repentance and forgiveness to those who sinned against You; and in the abundance of Your compassion, You decreed repentance for sinners, that they may be saved. Therefore, O Lord, God of the righteous, You appointed repentance, not for the righteous, not for Abraham and Isaac and Jacob who did not sin against You, but for me a sinner, for I committed more sins than there are grains of sand in the sea. My transgressions are multiplied, O Lord, they are multiplied! I am not worthy to look up and see the height of heaven because of the multitude of my iniquities, being weighed down by many iron chains so that I cannot raise my head; and there is no release for me because I have provoked Your anger and have done what is evil in Your sight, not doing Your will nor keeping Your commandment, but setting up abominations and multiplying offenses. Now I kneel in my heart, beseeching Your kindness: I have sinned, O Lord, I have sinned, and I acknowledge my transgressions; I pray and beg You; release me, Lord, release me! Do not destroy me together with my transgressions! Do not keep evils for me in anger forever! Do not condemn me to the depths of the earth! For You are God, the God of the repenting, and in me You will show all your kindness: for unworthy as I am You will save me according to the abundance of Your mercy, and I will praise You continually all the days of my life. For all the hosts of heaven sing Your praise, and Yours is the glory for ever and ever.

✠ ✠ ✠ ✠ ✠

Lord,
I have violated the law more than Manasseh;
I have lived more prodigally
than the prodigal son;
the enemy has taxed me
more than the publican;
I, who love prostitution,
have prostituted myself
more than the harlot;

I have sinned
more than Nineveh, but without repentance;
my sins have risen higher than my head,
and as a heavy burden
have pressed heavily upon me,
and thus, having become wretched,
I am utterly bowed down.
I have enraged Your holy Name;
I have distressed Your Holy Spirit;
I have despised Your commandments;
I have in various ways soiled my soul,
created in Your image;
I have wasted my life in sins,
the time that You gave me for repentance;
I have shamed my face;
I have totally blinded my eyes;
I have defiled my lips with lies;
and all the parts
of my soul and body
have been instruments of sin.
My mind
has been mingled with evil thoughts...
But, O Master,
look mercifully from Your holy high place,
behold my incorrigible soul
and with the means and ways You know
correct me by Your mercy.
As if standing before You, O Christ King,
as if touching Your immaculate feet,

so I implore You
with a broken heart.
Have mercy on me, O merciful One.

-St. Ephraim the Syrian

✦ ✦ ✦ ✦ ✦

O Lord and Master of my life,
take from me
the spirit of sloth, despair, lust of power and idle talk.
But give rather
the spirit of chastity, humility, patience,
and love to Your servant.
Yes, O Lord and King, grant to me to see my own sins,
and not to judge my sisters and brothers,
for You are blessed unto ages of ages.   Amen.

–The Lenten prayer of St. Ephraim the Syrian

✦ ✦ ✦ ✦ ✦

Try me, O God, and discern my paths;
see if there is a way of transgression in me,
and turn me away from it;
and lead me into the eternal way, O God,
You who have said,
"I am the way and the truth and the life," for You are
blessed unto the ages. Amen.

St. Macarius of Alexandria, 4th century

✦ ✦ ✦ ✦ ✦

O Jesus, the most-good goodness,
I have done no good before You;
but grant that I may make a beginning
because of Your goodness.

ST. NIKODEMOS OF THE HOLY MOUNTAIN

Psalm 51 (see page 15)

I, who am full of transgressions, judge those
who transgress.
If I am not honoured, I feel abhorred
and consider as enemies those who tell me the truth.
If I am not flattered, I feel disgusted.
Being unworthy, I accept honours.
Those who do not serve me I defame as arrogant.
I ignore the brother and sister who are sick,
but when I am sick,
I want to be loved and cared for.
I despise the superiors and overlook the inferiors.
If I keep myself even for a little bit
from unreasonable desires,
I become vainglorious.
If I attain some degree of vigilance,
I am entrapped by its opposite.
If I restrain myself from foods,
I am thrown down because of my pride.
If I make some progress in virtue,
I boast before my brothers and sisters.
Externally I appear humble,

but in my soul I am presumptuous.
I am not going to mention the vain thoughts I have in church,
and the wanderings of my mind during prayer.
I leave aside the hypocritical meetings,
the greed in the give and take of business,
and the publication of the mistakes of others
and the disastrous slanders.
This is my accursed life.
O Lord, grant me repentance
for the sake of Your infinite compassion.

ST. EPHRAIM THE SYRIAN, 4TH CENTURY

Look upon me in compassion, O God,
with Your merciful eyes and accept my
fervent confession.
Have mercy on me, O God, have mercy on me.

Instead of freedom from possessions, O Saviour,
I have pursued a life in love with material things;
and now I bear a heavy burden.
Have mercy on me, O God, have mercy on me.

Lord, You love humankind and desire that all should
be saved. In Your goodness call me back and accept
me in repentance. Have mercy on me, O God, have
mercy on me.

FROM THE GREAT CANON BY ST. ANDREW

Forgive Me, O God
O Lord Jesus Christ our God...
be merciful and forgive me, Your unworthy servant,
if somehow I have sinned this day as a human,
or rather as an inhuman.
Forgive my voluntary and involuntary sins,
the ones I have committed in knowledge or in
ignorance,
the ones that have been done
out of evil influences and carelessness
and my great indolence and negligence.
Forgive me, O Lord,
if I have taken an oath by Your holy name
or if I have violated my oath;
if I have sworn in my mind
or if I have somehow irritated You;
if I have stolen
or if I have lied;
if a friend came to me and I ignored him
or if I have distressed and embittered my brother;
if while standing in prayer and chanting,
my evil mind wandered off to evil and worldly things;
if I have delighted more than I should
or if I have said jokes,
and have laughed too much
or if I was vainglorious or proud;
if I looked upon vain beauty
and my mind was attracted by it;
if I was overly talkative about improper things

or if I busied myself with the faults of my brother
and condemned him
while overlooking my own innumerable faults;
if I have neglected my prayer
or if I have brought to mind any other evil thing.
Forgive me, O God,
your useless servant,
all these and whatever other things
I have done and do not remember.
Have mercy on me, O Lord,
for You are good and You love mankind,
so that I, the prodigal one,
may go to bed and fall asleep
glorifying you,
together with the Father
and your all-holy, good and life-creating Spirit,
now and ever and unto the ages of ages. Amen.

- ST. EPHRAIM THE SYRIAN

✢ ✢ ✢ ✢ ✢

I bless you, O Lord,
that You have worked wondrous mercies upon me, a sinner,
and have been most loving to me in all things:
nurse and governor,
guardian and helper,
refuge and saviour,
protector of both soul and body.
I bless You, O Lord,

for You have granted me the power to repent from my sins and have shown to me myriad occasions to return from my malice.

For You have mercy and save us, O God,

and to You we send up glory, thanksgiving and worship, together with Your only-begotten Son, and Your all-holy, good and life-creating Spirit, now and ever and unto the ages of ages. AMEN.

- ST. BASIL

For the Dying and the Departed

Blessed is the path thou goest on this day, for a place of rest is prepared for thee.

- ORTHODOX FUNERAL SERVICE

Your death, O Lord, became the cause of our immortality, because if You had not descended into the grave, Paradise would not have been opened to us. Therefore, give peace to this departed person for You love us all.

- ORTHODOX FUNERAL SERVICE

O God of spirits and all flesh, who has conquered death, overthrown the devil, and given life to Your world; give rest to the soul of Your servant (name), in a place of brightness, a place of freshness, a place of comfort, where there is no pain, sadness or longing. Pardon every transgression which he (she) has committed whether by word, deed or thought. For You are a good God who loves mankind. There is no one who lives and is sinless. For only You are without sin, and Your righteousness is eternal and Your Word is truth.   - ORTHODOX FUNERAL SERVICE

For You, O Christ our God, are the resurrection and the life and the comfort for Your servant (name). To You we ascribe glory, together with Your Father, who has always existed, and Your all-holy, good and life-giving Spirit, now and forever and to the ages of ages.
                                  - ORTHODOX FUNERAL SERVICE

Along with Your saints, O Christ, give rest to the soul of Your servant, in a place where there is neither pain, nor grief nor longing, but life everlasting.
                                  - ORTHODOX FUNERAL SERVICE

Lord, be mindful of Your servants (names), who have departed from this life in the hope of resurrection. Grant them forgiveness of sins, eternal rest among Your Saints, the gift of Your kingdom and the enjoyment of everlasting life with You. AMEN.
O Lord, we pray for our departed (name).
We believe, Lord, that whoever believes in You shall never die. Our loved ones are now with You in a special place You have prepared for them. We thank You

for the years they were with us. Now, they cannot come to us, but we will go to them. The separation is only temporary. We look forward to the day when we shall be reunited in your kingdom. We loved them, but You love them infinitely more. We relinquish them to Your greater love and care. May they rest safe in Your gentle bosom, safe in Your everlasting arms. Grant us, the survivors, the strength each day to endure and overcome the pain of grief. It is a pain we cannot escape but with Your help we shall pass through it and come away with greater empathy, understanding and sympathy. AMEN.

For One Who Is Dying

Receive in peace the soul this thy servant (name) and give him rest in thine eternal dwelling with all thy Saints, by the grace of thine only Son our Lord and God and Saviour, Jesus Christ, with whom thou art blessed together with thine all-holy, gracious and life-giving Spirit now and for ever and unto ages of ages. AMEN.

Prayer after the Departing of the Soul

Remember, O Lord, our God, this thy servant our brother (name) who now standeth before Thee in the faith and hope of eternal life. Release him from his sins, destroying his iniquity, pardoning, loosing and freeing him from all his transgressions, voluntary and involuntary. Save him from the eternal sufferings and fires of hell. Grant him to enjoy and to share in Thine eternal bliss which Thou hast prepared for all that love Thee: though he has sinned, yet has he not rejected Thee; confessing Thee faithfully even in his latest breath–the Father, the Son and the Holy Ghost, and believing in God glorified in the Holy Trinity, One in Three and Three in One, according to the Orthodox Faith. Be Thou therefore merciful to him, looking rather upon his faith than his works, and grant him rest with all Thy saints, for Thou art bountiful. No man who lives is without sin, and Thou alone art free from all stain, and Thy truth abideth for ever. Thou art the One merciful and bountiful God who lovest mankind, and to Thee we ascribe glory, to the Father and to the Son and to the Holy Ghost now and for ever and unto ages of ages. AMEN.

Commemoration of the Departed

Remember, O Lord, those who have departed this life: all Orthodox patriarchs, metropolitans, archbishops, bishops and all who served You in the priesthood and ministry of the Church and in the monastic order, and grant them rest with Your saints in Your eternal kingdom.

Remember, O Lord, the souls of Your servants now fallen asleep: our parents, family and friends. Forgive them all their sins, committed knowingly or unknowingly; grant them Your kingdom, a portion in Your eternal blessing and the enjoyment of Your unending life.

Remember, O Lord, all who have fallen asleep in the hope of the resurrection and of eternal life: our fathers, mothers, brothers, sisters and children, all our loved ones and Orthodox Christians throughout the world. Place them with Your saints before the light of Your countenance and have mercy on us, for You are good and love mankind.

(specific prayer requests for the departed
may be added here)

✛ ✛ ✛ ✛ ✛

I stretch out my arms to my Savior, who, after being foretold for four thousand years, came on earth to die and suffer for me at the time and circumstances foretold. By His grace I peaceably await death, in the hope of being eternally united to Him, and meanwhile I live joyfully, whether in the blessings which He is pleased to bestow on me or in the afflictions He may send me for my own good and taught me how to endure by His example.
Remember Lord,
our fathers and mothers, sisters and brothers
who have fallen asleep
in the hope of the resurrection to eternal life,
and all those who ended this life in piety and faith.

Pardon their every transgression,
committed voluntarily or involuntarily,
in word, or deed, or thought.
Bestow on them and on us your kingdom.
Grant them the participation of Your everlasting blessings,
and the enjoyment of Your endless life.
For You are the life, the resurrection and the peace
of Your departed servants, Christ our God,
and to You we give glory, together with Your all-holy, good, and life-giving Spirit,
now and forever and to the ages of ages.

ST. BASIL THE GREAT, 4TH CENTURY

Entering the Bridal Chamber

Dear Lord, our beloved (name) has entered the bridal chamber of Your glory where the rejoicing of the celebrants and the unspeakable delight of those who behold the ineffable beauty of Your countenance never ceases. Glory to You.

Christ is Risen: Personalized

Christ is risen from the dead.
By His death He has destroyed death.
To those in the tombs and to His beloved
servant (name),
He has bestowed life.
Glory to You, our Risen Lord.

Asleep in the Hope of the Resurrection

Lord, remember Your servant (name) who has fallen asleep in the hope of the resurrection. Forgive him (her) every transgression he (she) has committed in thought, word or deed. Grant him (her) peace and refreshment in a place of light where Your glory delights all the Saints. For You are the resurrection, the repose and the life of Your departed servant (name), and to You I give glory, now and forever. AMEN.

The Death of a Loved One

Dear Tender Shepherd, the one I loved is gone, the funeral over, friends and relatives have departed. Now it is my task to write and to visit insurers, employers, and government officials; to give away or put away possessions; to begin anew. Be with me when so many things remind me of recent sorrow and earlier joys. As You once wept with your friends, so may I not be ashamed of my feelings during this time of remembering, when a picture, a letter or a card may bring alive another time. Thank You for the special memories of warmth and joy and for the promise that You will always be by my side. AMEN.

Prayers of Praise and Doxology

The Grace
(2 Corinthians 13:14)
May the grace of the Lord Jesus Christ,
and the love of God,
and the fellowship of the Holy Spirit,
be with you all.

A Doxology from Paul
(Ephesians 3:20-21)
Now to Him who is able to do immeasurably more than all we ask or imagine, according to His power that is at work within us, to Him be glory in the church and in Christ Jesus throughout all generations, for ever and ever! Amen.

Songs of Praise from "Revelation"
You are worthy, our Lord and our God,
to receive glory and honour and power,
for You created all things,
and by Your will they were created and have their being.

Worthy is the Lamb, who was slain,
to receive power and wealth and wisdom and strength
and honour and glory and praise!
To Him who sits on the throne and to the Lamb

be praise and honour and glory and power,
for ever and ever!

Amen!
Praise and glory
and wisdom and thanks and honour
and power and strength
be to our God for ever and ever.
Amen!

✠✠✠✠✠

Great are You, O Lord,
and wondrous are your works,
and no word will suffice to sing Your wonders.
For You by your will
have out of nothingness brought all things into being
and by Your power sustain all creation,
and by Your providence direct the world.
You from the four elements have formed creation
and have crowned the cycle of the year with the four
seasons.
All the spiritual powers tremble before You;
the sun praises You; the moon glorifies You;
the stars in their courses meet with You;
the light hearkens unto You;
the depths shudder at Your presence;
the springs of water serve You.
You have stretched out the heavens as a curtain;
You have founded the earth upon the waters;

You have bounded the sea with sand;
You have poured forth the air for breathing;
the angelic powers minister unto You.
The cherubim and the seraphim,
as they stand and fly around You
veil themselves with fear of Your
unapproachable glory.
For You,
being boundless and beginningless and unutterable,
came down on earth,
taking the form of a servant,
being made in human likeness.
For You, O Master, through the tenderness
of Your mercy,
could not endure the human race tormented by
the devil,
but You came and saved us.
We confess Your grace;
we proclaim Your beneficence;
we do not hide Your mercy.
You have set free our mortal nature.
All creation sings praises to You
who have revealed Yourself.
For You, our God, have appeared upon earth
and have dwelt among us.
You have sanctified the Jordan streams...

EXCERPT FROM THE GREAT BLESSING OF WATER

Praise the Lord, all works of the Lord.
Praise the Lord, you heavens, you angels of the Lord.
Praise the Lord, all waters above the heavens.
Praise the Lord, all powers.
Praise the Lord, sun and moon, stars of heaven.
Praise the Lord, all rain and dew, all winds.
Praise the Lord, sing and exalt Him
throughout all the ages.
Praise the Lord, fire and heat,
cold and summer heat,
dews and snows.
Praise the Lord, nights and days, light and darkness.
Praise the Lord, ice and cold, frosts and snows.
Praise the Lord, lightnings and clouds.
Praise the Lord, sing and exalt Him
throughout all the ages.

Let the earth bless the Lord.
Praise the Lord, mountains and hills,
all things that grow on the earth.
Praise the Lord, you springs, seas and rivers.
Praise the Lord, you whales
and all the creatures that move in the waters.
Praise the Lord, all birds of the air, all beasts
and cattle.
Praise the Lord, sing and exalt Him through
all the ages.
Praise the Lord, you sons and daughters of men.
Praise the Lord, O Israel.

Praise the Lord, you priests of the Lord.
Praise the Lord, you servants of the Lord.
Praise the Lord, spirits and souls of the righteous.
Praise the Lord, you who are holy and humble
in heart.
Praise the Lord, Ananiah, Azariah and Mishael.
Praise the Lord, apostles, prophets and martyrs
of the Lord.
We praise the Father, the Son and the Holy Spirit.
Now and ever, and unto ages of ages. Amen.
We praise, bless and worship the Lord,
singing and exalting Him throughout the ages.

VESPER HYMN, HOLY SATURDAY, FROM THE
HYMN OF THE THREE YOUTH IN THE BOOK OF DANIEL
ACCORDING TO THE SEPTUAGINT

Te Deum

You are God and we praise You; You are the Lord
and we acclaim you;
You are the eternal Father; all creation worships You.
To You all angels, all the powers of heaven,
Cherubim and Seraphim sing in endless praise,
Holy holy holy Lord, God of power and might;
Heaven and earth are full of your glory.
The glorious company of apostles praise You;
The noble fellowship of prophets praise You;
The white-robed army of martyrs praise You.
Throughout the whole world the holy church
acclaims You,

Father of majesty unbounded;
Your true and only Son worthy of all worship,
And the Holy Spirit advocate and guide.
You Christ are the King of glory,
The eternal Son of the Father.
When You became man to set us free
You did not abhor the virgin's womb.
You overcame the sting of death
And opened the kingdom of heaven to all believers.
You are seated at God's right hand in glory;
We believe that You will come and be our judge.
Come then Lord and help Your people,
Bought with the price of Your own blood;
And bring us with Your saints
To glory everlasting.

–A PRAYER FROM THE FOURTH CENTURY

For Joy and Gladness

The Clementine Liturgy
(First Century)

Blessed art Thou, O Lord, who hast nourished me from my youth up, who givest food to all flesh. Fill our hearts with joy and gladness, that we, always having all sufficiency in all things, may abound to every good work in Christ Jesus our Lord, through whom to Thee be glory, honour, might, majesty, and dominion, forever and ever. AMEN.

✠ ✠ ✠ ✠ ✠

I glorify the power of the Father,
I magnify the power of the Son,
and I sing a hymn of praise to the power of the
Holy Spirit;
one Godhead,
Trinity, indivisible, uncreated,
equal in essence and reigning forever.

HYMN OF THE RESURRECTION

✤ ✤ ✤ ✤ ✤

The poor and the needy will praise you, O Lord.
Glory to the Father,
glory to the Son,
glory to the Holy Spirit, who spoke
through the prophets.
God is my hope,
Christ is my refuge,
the Holy Spirit is my shelter.

ST. AUXENTIOS, 3RD CENTURY

The Magnificat
(Luke 1:46-55)

Refrain:
More honorable than the cherubim
And more glorious beyond compare
than the seraphim!
Without corruption you gave birth to God the Word.

True Theotokos, we magnify you!
My soul magnifies the Lord, and my spirit has rejoiced in God my Savior.

For He has regarded the lowly state of His maidservant; for behold, henceforth, all generations will call me blessed.

For He who is mighty has done great things for me, and holy is His name. And His mercy is on those who fear Him from generation to generation.

He has shown strength with His arm; he has scattered the proud in the imagination of their hearts.

Doxology
Glory to God, Who has shown us the Light!

Glory to God in the highest, and on earth, peace, good will toward men!

We praise You! We bless You! We worship You! We glorify You and give thanks to You for Your great glory!

O Lord God, Heavenly King, God the Father Almighty!

O Lord, the Only-Begotten Son, Jesus Christ, and the Holy Spirit!

O Lord God, Lamb of God, Son of the Father, Who take away the sins of the world, have mercy on us!

You, Who take away the sins of the world, receive our prayer!

You, Who sit on the right hand of God the Father, have mercy on us!

For You alone are holy, and You alone are Lord. You alone, O Lord Jesus Christ, are most high in the glory of God the Father! Amen!

I will give thanks to You every day and praise Your Name for ever and ever.

Lord, You have been our refuge from generation to generation! I said, "Lord, have mercy on me. Heal my soul, for I have sinned against You!"

Lord, I flee to You. Teach me to do Your will, for You are my God. For with You is the fountain of Life, and in Your light shall we see light. Continue Your lovingkindness to those who know You.

Vouchsafe, O Lord, to keep us this day without sin.

Blessed are you, O Lord, the God of our fathers, and praised and glorified is Your Name for ever. Amen.

Let Your mercy be upon us, O Lord, even as we have set our hope on You.

Blessed are You, O Lord; teach me Your statutes.
Blessed are You, O Master; make me to understand Your commandments.
Blessed are You, O Holy One; enlighten me with Your precepts.

Your mercy endures for ever, O Lord! Do not despise the works of Your hands!

To You belongs worship. To You belongs praise. To You belongs glory: to the Father and to the Son and the Holy Spirit; now and ever and unto ages of ages. AMEN.

Psalm148
Praise the Lord! Praise the Lord from the heavens; praise Him in the heights!
Praise Him, all His angels; praise Him, all His hosts!
Praise Him, sun and moon; praise Him, all you stars of light!
Praise Him, you heavens and you waters above the heavens!

Let them praise the name of the Lord, for He commanded and they were created.

He has also established them forever and ever; He has made a decree which shall not pass away.

Praise the Lord from the earth, you great sea creatures and all the depths;

Fire and hail, snow and clouds; stormy wind, fulfilling His word;

Mountains and all hills; fruitful trees and all cedars;

Beasts and all cattle; creeping things and flying fowl;

Kings of the earth and all peoples; princes and all judges of the earth;

Both young men and maidens; old men and children.

Let them praise the name of the Lord, for His name alone is exalted; His glory is above the earth and heaven.

And He has exalted the horn of His people, the praise of all His saints – of the children of Israel, a people near to Him. Praise the Lord!

✠ ✠ ✠ ✠ ✠

I bless You, O Lord.

Though I am powerless, You strengthen my weakness.

You stretch from above Your helping hand
and bring me back unto myself.

What shall I render to You, O all-good Master,
for all the good things You have done

and continue to do for me,
the sinner?
I will cease not to bless You all the days of my life,
my creator,
my benefactor
and my guardian.

ST. BASIL THE GREAT, 4TH CENTURY

Lord, my God,
You are great, fearful and glorious,
the creator of every visible and spiritual creation.
You are faithful to your covenant and mercy,
for those who love you and keep Your
commandments.
I thank You both now and forever
for all the blessings, seen and unseen,
that have been bestowed upon me.
Even up to this present time,
I praise, glorify and magnify You,
for everything
that has proven Your rich mercy and compassion
to be wondrous in me,
helping me, out of your goodness and love for
humankind, from my mother's womb
and providing in every way
to protect and to govern in a holy manner
the matters of my life.

ST. JOHN CHRYSOSTOM, 4TH CENTURY

✝ ✝ ✝ ✝ ✝

How many times, after I had sinned,
You comforted me, as a good Father,
and You kissed me warmly as a son or a daughter,
and You stretched out Your arms to me and cried out:
rise up, fear not, stand up, come!

ST. JOHN OF DAMASCUS, 7TH-8TH CENTURY

Lenten Prayers

A Lenten Prayer by St. Effrem the Syrian

O Lord and Master of my life!
Take away from me the will
to be lazy and to be sad;
The desire to get ahead
of other people and
to boast and brag.

Give me instead a pure and
humble spirit,
The will to be patient
with other people
and to love them.

O Lord and King, let me
realize my own sins
And keep me from judging

what other people do,
For You are blessed
now and forever. AMEN.

Lenten Prayer from the Liturgy of the Presanctified Gifts

Almighty God, Who made all creation in wisdom
    and by your inexpressible providence
        and goodness
    has brought us to these holy days for the purifica-
        tion of body and soul,
    for the controlling of bodily passions,
    for the hope of the Resurrection,
Who, during the forty days gave the Covenant into
    the hands of Moses in characters divinely traced
    by You:
    Enable us also, O Holy One,
    to fight the good fight;
    to accomplish the course of this fast;
    to preserve in wholeness the faith;
    to crush under foot the heads of invisible
        serpents;
    to be counted a victor over sin;
    and so uncondemned to attain the holy
        resurrection.
    For all honor and glory is given to your noble
        and worthy Name,
    Father, Son and Holy Spirit
    now and always and forever and ever. Amen.

Short "Breath" Prayers

In the context of our verbose culture it is significant to hear the Desert Fathers discouraging us from using too many words: "Abba Macarius was asked 'How should one pray?' The old man said, 'There is no need at all to make long discourses; it is enough to stretch out one's hand and say, 'Lord, as you will, as you know, have mercy.' And if the conflict grows fiercer, say: 'Lord, help.' He knows very well what we need and he shows us His mercy."

John Climacus is even more explicit: "When you pray do not try to express yourself in fancy words, for often it is the simple, repetitious phrases of a little child that our Father in heaven finds most irresistible. Do not strive for verbosity lest your mind be distracted from devotion by a search for words. One phrase on the lips of the tax collector was enough to win God's mercy; one humble request made with faith was enough to save the good thief. Wordiness in prayer often subjects the mind to fantasy and dissipation; single words of their very nature tend to concentrate the mind. When you find satisfaction or compunction in a certain word of your prayer, stop at that point."

This is a very helpful suggestion for us, people who depend so much on verbal ability. The quiet repetition of a single word can help us to descend with the mind into the heart.

The hesychastic tradition of the Church has developed what is usually called aspiratory prayer or breath prayer. It is a short, simple prayer that can be spoken in one breath. A breath prayer by consistent repetition serves to focus the mind on God. The most famous of the breath prayers is the Jesus Prayer. Gregory of Sinai said, "One's love of God should run before breathing."

The Jesus Prayer
Based on the words of the blind beggar healed by Jesus, this prayer has traditionally been used as a basis for meditation by Orthodox Christians.

Lord Jesus Christ, Son of God,
have mercy on me the sinner!
or, "Lord, have mercy"
or, "Lord Jesus"
or, "Jesus Christ"
or, "Jesus"

Prayer for Protection
This inscription was found on a Christian house in Asia Minor:
May the Lord of the powers in His mercy protect us as we go in and out.

Lord of Hosts: A Prayer to Jesus

O Lord of Hosts,
You suffered and rose,
Appeared and ascended
And will come to judge the world.
We fall down before You...   - PRAYER OF THE TENTH HOUR

Prayer to the Trinity

My hope is the Father
My refuge is the Son
My protection is the Holy Spirit
Blessed Trinity, glory to Thee.

Turn to me and be gracious to me, for I am lonely and afflicted. Relieve the troubles of my heart, and bring me out of my distress (Ps. 25).

Personalizing John 3:16

God so loved the world and me (your name) that He gave His only begotten Son so that I (your name) who believes in Him might not perish but have life everlasting.

Created-Redeemed-Indwelt

I am loved by God the Father Who created me out of nothing. I am loved and redeemed by God the Son, my Precious Jesus, who loved me and gave Himself for me. I am loved and indwelt by God the Holy

Spirit, God's power and presence within me. Blessed Trinity, glory to You.
Glory be to the Father and to the Son and to the Holy Spirit now and forevermore. AMEN.

✚ ✚ ✚ ✚ ✚

God be merciful to me the sinner.

✚ ✚ ✚ ✚ ✚

By the prayers of the Most Holy Theotokos and of all the saints, Lord Jesus Christ have mercy on me.

✚ ✚ ✚ ✚ ✚

O Lord, baptize me with love.
Jesus, teach me gentleness.
Gracious Master, remove my fear.
Holy Spirit, reveal my sin.
Lord Jesus, help me feel loved.

Prayers from the Akathist Hymn to our Sweetest Lord Jesus

Jesus, invincible strength,
Jesus, boundless mercy,
Jesus, unsurpassable in beauty,
Jesus, unspeakable in love,
Jesus, Son of the Living God,
Jesus, have mercy on me, a sinner.

✢ ✢ ✢ ✢ ✢

Jesus, Uncontrollable Word!
Jesus, Inscrutable Intelligence!
Jesus, Incomprehensible Power!
Jesus, Inconceivable Wisdom!
Jesus, Boundless Dominion!
Jesus, Supreme Strength!
Jesus, Eternal Power!
Jesus, my Savior, save me!

✢ ✢ ✢ ✢ ✢

Jesus, True God!
Jesus, Glorious King!
Jesus, Innocent Lamb!
Jesus, Wonderful Shepherd!

Jesus, my Hope at death!
Jesus, my Life after death!
Jesus, my Comfort at Thy Judgement!
Jesus, Son of God, have mercy on me!

✠ ✠ ✠ ✠ ✠

Jesus, Most Wonderful, Forefathers' deliverance!
Jesus, Most Sweet, Patriarchs' Exaltation!
Jesus, Most Beloved, Prophets' Fulfillment!
Jesus, Most Marvelous, Martyrs' Strength!
Jesus, Most Tender, Saints' Rejoicing!
Jesus, Everlasting, Sinners' Salvation!
Jesus, Son of God, have mercy on me!

✠ ✠ ✠ ✠ ✠

Jesus, the Truth, dispelling falsehood!
Jesus, the Light above all lights!
Jesus, the King, surpassing all in strength!
Jesus, the Bread of Life.
Jesus, Source of Knowledge.
Jesus, Garment of Gladness.
Jesus, Veil of Joy.
Jesus, Giver to those who ask.
Jesus, Opener to those who knock.
Jesus, Redeemer of sinners.
Jesus, Son of God, have mercy on me!
"Christ hungered as man, and fed the hungry as God.

He was hungry as man, and yet He is the Bread
of Life;
He was athirst as a man, and yet He says, 'Let him
that is athirst come unto Me and drink';
He was weary, and yet He is our rest;
He pays tribute, and yet He is a King;
He prays, and yet hears prayer;
He weeps, and dries our tears;
He is sold for thirty pieces of silver, and
redeems the world;
He is 'led as a sheep to the slaughter,'
and is the Good Shepherd;
He is mute as a sheep, and yet He is the everlasting
Word."

✠ ✠ ✠ ✠ ✠

Jesus, Sweetness of the heart!
Jesus, Strength of the Body!
Jesus, Purity of the soul!
Jesus, Brightness of the mind!
Jesus, Gladness of the conscience!
Jesus, Son of God, have mercy on me!

✠ ✠ ✠ ✠ ✠

Jesus, King of peace, bestow Thy peace upon me.
Jesus, sweet-scented Flower, make me fragrant.
Jesus, longed-for Warmth, warm Thou me.
Jesus, eternal Temple, shelter me.

Jesus, resplendent Garment, adorn me.

Jesus, Pearl of great price, enrich me.

Jesus, Precious Stone, illumine me.

Jesus, Sun of righteousness, shine on me.

Jesus, Holy Light, make me radiant.

Jesus, deliver me from infirmity of soul and body.

Jesus, rescue me from the hands of the adversary.

Jesus, save me from the everlasting torments.

Jesus, Son of God, have mercy on me.

Jesus, Creator of those on high.

Jesus, Redeemer of those below.

Jesus, Vanquisher of the nethermost powers.

Jesus, Adorner of every creature.

Jesus, Comforter of my soul.

Jesus, Enlightener of my mind.

Jesus, Gladness of my heart.

Jesus, Health of my body.

Jesus, my Saviour, save me.

Jesus, my Light, enlighten me.

Jesus, from all torment deliver me.

Jesus, save me who am unworthy.

Jesus, Son of God, have mercy on me. *

* For the complete service we refer you to *The Service of Preparation for Holy Communion with Akathist to Our Saviour and the Theotokos* available through Light & Life Publishing Company

Prayers to Jesus

Christ our God,
sun of righteousness,
by Your divine touch
You gave light to the eyes of the blind man
who had been deprived of light since birth.
Enlighten also the eyes of our souls,
and make us sons and daughters of light
so that we may cry out to You in faith:
great and beyond words is Your compassion
towards us!
Loving Lord, glory to You!

Vesper Hymn, Sunday of the Blind Man

Eternal Son and Word of God, spring of healings,
You found the Samaritan woman by Jacob's well
and asked her for water.
What a wonder!
He who is enthroned upon the cherubim
speaks with a sinful woman.
He who has set the earth upon the waters
 asks for water.
He who pours forth fountains of waters
asks her who was caught in the snares of the adversary
for water that He may draw her to Him.
He Who is merciful
seeks to give living water to her who is burning
with sins.

Therefore let us praise Him
Loving Lord, glory to You!

VESPER HYMNS, SUNDAY OF THE SAMARITAN WOMAN

✠ ✠ ✠ ✠ ✠

Let there be no gap between us and Christ.
Of if there is any gap, immediately we perish.
For the building stands because it is cemented
together.
Let us not then merely keep hold of Christ,
    but let us be cemented to Him.
Let us cleave to Him by our works.
He is the head, we are the body.
He is the foundation, we the building.
He is the vine, we the branches.
He is the bridegroom, we the bride.
He is the shepherd, we the sheep.
He is the way, we walk in it.
Again, we are the temple, He the indweller.
He is the only begotten, we the brothers and sisters.
He is the heir, we the heirs together with Him.
He is the life, we the living.
He is the resurrection, we those who rise again.
He is the light, we the enlightened.

HOMILIES ON FIRST CORINTHIANS,
ST. JOHN CHRYSOSTOM, 4TH CENTURY

Christ, our God,
who has made it possible for us to pray together
and who promised that
when two or three are gathered in Your name
You will give what they ask:
Fulfill now our request,
insofar as it is good and according to the special
needs of each,
granting us in his world the knowledge of Your truth
and in the world to come eternal life.
For You are a loving God
and to You we give glory,
to the Father and the Son and the Holy Spirit,
now and forever. AMEN.

ST. JOHN CHRYSOSTOM LITURGY

Christ, our Lord,
You have abolished the curse of sin by Your cross.
You have done away with the power of death by
Your burial.
You have illumined humanity by your resurrection.
Therefore, we cry out to You:
glory to You, O Christ, our Lord and benefactor!

RESURRECTION HYMN

✦ ✦ ✦ ✦ ✦

The Lord is everything to me.
  He is the strength of my heart,
  and the light of my mind.
He inclines my heart to everything good;
He strengthens it:
He also gives me good thoughts.
  He is my rest and my joy;
  He is my faith, hope and love.
He is my food and drink,
my raiment, my dwelling place.

ST. JOHN OF KRONDSTADT, 19TH CENTURY

Prayers for Married Persons

O Lord Jesus Christ, thank You for blessing
  our marriage through the Sacrament of
  Holy Matrimony.
When we stood together before Your Holy Altar,
  we invited You to come and bless us.
We claim Your Holy Presence in our marriage
  this day and every day.
You are the Source of Love.
Keep pouring Your love into us through the
  Holy Spirit.
Help us to stay close to You.
Help us to prefer one another in love,

To consider it a privilege to be able to serve
    one another
'Til we see You face to face.
Help us to be kind to each other, tenderhearted,
Forgiving one another as You have forgiven us.
Never let the sun go down on our anger.
Grant us always to see our own faults
And not to judge each other.
Open our eyes to the best in each other.
Let patience reign supreme in our hearts.
Give us hope to brighten life,
And joy to lighten sorrow.

May our home be a haven where spiritual
    values are treasured and
Holy principles are modeled.
Gladden us with Your grace and peace
    that with one heart we may
Praise and glorify You. AMEN.

✠ ✠ ✠ ✠ ✠

For My Husband

Dear Lord, I am so blessed to be married to the man I call my husband. "Husband" just doesn't seem to convey all that he is to me. He is my lover, my best friend, my confidant, my companion. There's no one else I'd rather laugh or cry with–in good times or bad. How grateful I am that You have brought us together.

Yet I am only human, Lord. Sometimes I get angry or
upset at something he has said or done–or *hasn't* said
or done–and I lose my patience and my temper.
Sometimes I concentrate on the qualities or habits I
wish I could change rather than on his best qualities
and endearing habits. Lord, at those times, help me to
remember why I love him so much and to let go of the
rest. Amen.

✠ ✠ ✠ ✠ ✠

Praying with a Prayer Rope

Many Orthodox monks use a prayer rope to assist
them in following their daily rule of prayer. The color
of the rope is black, the appropriate color of mourning and sorrow for our sins. The prayer most often
used with the prayer rope is the Jesus Prayer which is
a plea for God's mercy on the sinner.

The prayer rope is made of wool. This serves to
remind us that we are the rational sheep of the Good
Shepherd, and that Jesus is the Lamb of God Who
takes away the sins of the world. Most prayer ropes
have a cross woven into them at the end.

Prayer ropes come in a variety of forms and sizes,
and also have some kind of marker after each 33, 50,
or 100 knots.

The prayer rope is one of the items given to an
Orthodox monk at the time of tonsure. It is given as a

form of spiritual sword with which he is to do battle with the spiritual enemy. The power of this sword lies in the Jesus Prayer which may be used either in its complete form or many shorter forms:

"Lord Jesus Christ, Son of the Living God,
    have mercy on me the sinner."

"Lord Jesus Christ, have mercy on me."

"Lord have mercy."

"Kyrie eleison."

"Lord Jesus Christ."

"Lord Jesus."

"Jesus."

For other short prayers that may be used with the prayer rope, see the section in this book on "Breath Prayers."

Monks carry the prayer rope with them to remind them of their obligation to pray unceasingly. It can be used as such by Orthodox lay people as well. Carried in a purse or pocket, the prayer rope will remind us to practice our daily rule of prayer. Placed over the head of our bed, or in our automobile, it can serve to bring the blessing of God's holy presence into our lives.

The prayer rope can be used to pray some of the prayers in this book as one slowly begins to establish one's own personal daily rule of prayer. It can also be used to pray the Jesus Prayer a specific number of times each day.

The prayer rope will serve as a daily reminder and invitation to pray. It will give you something important to do while you are commuting or traveling or waiting for appointments in the doctor's office or elsewhere.

Many people take the prayer rope to bed with them at night. Signing their bed with the cross, they bless themselves with the sign of the cross and pray quietly, prayer rope in hand, until they fall asleep. Waking up the next morning with the same prayer rope in hand, they immediately greet the new day with praise and glory to God. If they should pass into the Eternal Day while at sleep, what better way to enter God's presence than with a prayer rope in hand!

---

* If you wish to purchase a prayer rope, write or call:

Light & Life Publishing Company, P.O. Box 26421, Minneapolis, MN 55426. Telephone: 1-(952)-925-3888

Prayers of Exorcism Against the Devil

by St. John Chrysostom (344-407A.D.)

O Eternal God, who has redeemed us from the captivity of the Devil, deliver Your servant (Name) from all the workings of unclean spirits. Command the evil and impure spirits and demons to depart from the soul and body of Your servant (name) and not to remain nor hide in him. Let them be banished from this creation of Your hands in Your own holy Name and that of Your only begotten Son and of Your life-giving Spirit, so that, after being cleansed from all demonic influence, he may live godly, justly and righteously and may be counted worthy to receive the Holy Mysteries of Your only-begotten Son and our God with whom You are blessed and glorified together with the all-holy and good and life-giving Spirit now and ever and unto the ages of ages. AMEN.

✤✤✤✤✤

The Lord rebukes you, Devil!–He who calls forth the water of the sea and pours it upon the face of all the earth. Lord of Hosts in his Name. Devil: the Lord rebukes you! He who is ministered and praised by numberless heavenly orders and adored and glorified in fear by multitudes of angelic and archangelic hosts.

Satan: the Lord rebukes you! He who is honored by the encircling Powers, the awesome six-winged and many-eyed Cherubim and Seraphim that cover their faces with two wings because of his inscrutable and unseen divinity and with two wings cover their feet, lest they be seared by his inutterable glory and incomprehensible majesty, and with two wings do fly and fill the heavens with their shouts of "Holy, holy, holy, Lord Sabaoth, heaven and earth are full of your glory!"

✠ ✠ ✠ ✠ ✠

Devil: The Lord rebukes you! He who came down from the Father's bosom and through the holy, inexpressible, immaculate and adorable Incarnation from the Virgin, appeared ineffably in the world to save it and cast you down from heaven in his authoritative power and showed you an outcast to every man.

✠ ✠ ✠ ✠ ✠

Satan: The Lord rebukes you! He who said to the sea, Be silent, be still, and instantly was calmed at His command. Devil: The Lord rebukes you! He who made clay with his immaculate spittle and refashioned the man blind from birth and gave him his sight.

✠ ✠ ✠ ✠ ✠

Depart swiftly from this creature of the Creator Christ our God! And be gone from the servant of God (name), from his mind, from his soul, from his heart, from his reins, from his senses, from all his members, that he might become whole and sound and free, knowing God, his own Master and Creator of all things, Him who gathers together those who have gone astray and who gives them the seal of salvation through the rebirth and restoration of divine baptism, so that he may be counted worthy of the immaculate, heavenly and awesome Mysteries and be united to his true fold, dwelling in a place of pasture and nourished on the waters of repose, guided pastorally and safely by the staff of the Cross unto the forgiveness of sins and life everlasting.

For to Him belong all glory, honor, adoration and majesty together with Your beginningless Father and His all-holy, good and life-giving Spirit, now and ever, and unto ages of ages. AMEN.

Prayer in the Time of Trouble

O God, You are my Rock and my Salvation,
    To You I cling during this dark hour
    of tribulation.
Hold my hand tightly, for I lack even that little

strength I need to hold on to Your Hand.
Have mercy on me, Lord, and deliver me
    from the trouble that besets me.
I acknowledge that I deserve any
    chastisement that comes to me,
For I know I have sinned, O Lord.
Do not deal with me according to my sins,
But according to Your bountiful mercy.
For I am the work of Your hands.
You know my weakness.
You remember that I am but dust.
Grant me strength to endure my
    tribulation with complete trust in You.

As You came to Peter and the other disciples
    late one stormy night on the Sea of Galilee to
    quell the storm and restore calm,
Quell the storm that rages in my soul.
Take away all fear and anxiety.
Fill me with Your peace.
Grant that this trial may bring
    me closer to You.
For You are my strength, my hope and
    my joy.
Blessed is Your Name always Father, Son, and
    Holy Spirit. AMEN.

Prayer for a Sick Person

Heavenly Father, Who sent Your only-begotten
    Son, our Lord Jesus Christ, to be the
    Physician of our souls and bodies,
Who came to heal sickness and infirmity,
Who healed the paralytic,
And brought back to life the daughter of Jairus,
Who healed the woman who had been
    sick for twelve years
By her mere touch of the hem of Your robe,
Visit and heal also Your beloved
    servant (name) from all physical
    and spiritual maladies
    by the power and grace of Your Christ.
Grant (name) the patience that comes from
    believing that You are always at work in our
    lives to bring good out of evil.
Grant (name) strength of body, mind, and soul.
Raise him/her up from the bed of pain.
Grant him/her full recovery.
May (name) experience the same surge of
    healing power flow through his/her body
    as did
The sick woman who touched Your robe,
For we, too, are touching Your robe today,
    dear Lord, through this our prayer.
We approach You with the same faith as
    she did.

Grant (name) the gift of health.
For You alone are the source of healing.
To You we offer glory, praise and thanksgiving,
    Father, Son and Holy Spirit. AMEN.

Intercessory Prayers

O Lord Jesus Christ our God, who in Your mercy and
loving-kindness, hears the prayers of all who call upon
You with their whole heart, incline Your ear and hear
my prayer, now humbly offered unto You:

Make our supplication acceptable to You;
Grant the remission of our sins;
Protect us under the shelter of Your wings;
Drive away from us every enemy and adversary; and
preserve our lives in peace.
O Lord, have mercy on us and on all Your world, and
save our souls, for You are merciful, and You love
mankind.
Let us pray for the peace of the world;
For all pious and Orthodox Christians;
For the welfare and strengthening of our
Armed Forces;
For our Archbishop (name), our Bishop (name),
 and all the clergy and laity;
For our absent fathers and brethren;
For those who serve and have ministered unto us;

For those who enjoin us in our unworthiness to
pray for them;
For the release of captives;
For those who travel by land, sea, or air;
For those who live in sickness;
Let us pray also for the abundance of the fruits
of the earth;
For all our departed fathers and brethren, those that
peacefully lie here, and the Orthodox everywhere;
For the young and the old; orphans and widows;
the sorrowing, the afflicted, and the needy poor;
For me, Your humble servant; grant me Your grace
that I may be a faithful disciple,
leading a godly and righteous life, blameless and
peaceful, ever serving You that I may be found worthy
to enter into Your heavenly Kingdom;

(personal intercessions may be added at this point).

And let us say for ourselves: Lord have mercy, Lord
have mercy, Lord have mercy.
Hear my prayer, O Lord, for Thou art merciful and
compassionate, and lovest mankind, and to Thee are
due all glory, honor, and worship: to the Father and to
the Son, and the Holy Spirit; now and ever, and unto
ages of ages. AMEN.

✤ ✤ ✤ ✤ ✤

We, your servants, offer You, O God, prayers
and intercessions on behalf of the peace
of the churches and the tranquility
of the monasteries;
keep your ministers in righteousness,
forgive sinners who turn to You,
make the rich rich in almsgiving,
provide for the poor,
support the widows,
educate the orphans,
sustain the aged,
guard the youth by Your cross,
gather the dispersed,
convert those in error;

and let our prayers and intercessions prevail
with You,
and we will offer praise and honour
to Your high Trinity, now and always and forever.
AMEN.

–FROM THE SYRIAN LITURGY

For All Kings and Rulers
Clement of Rome
First Century

Grant unto all Kings and Rulers, O Lord, health,
peace, concord, and stability, that they may administer the government which Thou has given them without failure. For Thou, O heavenly Master, King of the

Ages, givest to the sons of men glory and honour, and power over all things that are upon the earth. Do Thou, Lord, direct their counsel according to that which is good and well pleasing in Thy sight, that administering in peace and gentleness, with godliness, the power which Thou has given them, they may obtain Thy favour. O Thou Who alone art able to do these things, and things far more exceeding good than these, for us, we praise Thee, through the High Priest and Guardian of our souls Jesus Christ; through Whom be the glory and the majesty, unto Thee, both now and for all generations, and forever and ever. AMEN.

✠ ✠ ✠ ✠ ✠

Give perfection to beginners, O Father; give intelligence to the little ones; give aid to those who are running their course. Give sorrow to the negligent; give fervor of spirit to the lukewarm. Give to the perfect a good consummation; for the sake of Christ Jesus our Lord. AMEN.   IRENAEUS, SECOND CENTURY

✠ ✠ ✠ ✠ ✠

Lord, bless those who praise You
and sanctify those who trust in You.
Save your people and bless Your inheritance.
Protect the whole body of Your church.
Sanctify those who love the beauty of Your house.

Glorify them in return by Your divine power,
and do not forsake us who hope in You.
Grant peace to Your world,
to Your churches, to the clergy,
to those in public service, and to all Your people.
For every good and perfect gift is from above,
coming from You, the Father of lights.
To You we give glory, thanksgiving and worship,
to the Father and the Son and the Holy Spirit,
now and forever and to the ages of ages. Amen.

LITURGY OF ST. JOHN CHRYSOSTOM

✦ ✦ ✦ ✦ ✦

From the Liturgy of Basil the Great

We beseech Thee, O Lord, remember Thy Holy Catholic and Apostolic Church, from one end of the world unto the other, and give peace unto it, which Thou hast purchased with the precious Blood of Thy Christ, and strengthen this holy House till the consummation of the world. Remember, O Lord, those who have offered their holy gifts unto Thee, and those for whom, or for what ends they have offered them. Remember, O Lord, those who bring forth fruit, and do good works in Thy Holy Churches and who remember the poor...Remember, O Lord, the people who stand around, and those who are absent and have mercy upon them and upon us, according to the multitude of Thy mercy...Remember O Lord, those that are in trials and banishments, and all tribulation and necessity and distress and all that need Thy great loving kindness. Free those troubled by unclean spirits; sail with them that sail; journey with travellers; protect widows and orphans, deliver the captives, and heal the sick...Pour out on all Thy rich mercy, granting to all their petitions unto salvation. And those whom we, through ignorance, or forgetfulness, or the number of names, have not remembered, do Thou, O God, remember them, who knowest the age and the name of each one, who knowest each from his mother's womb. For Thou, O God, art the Help of the helpless, the Hope of the hopeless, the Saviour of the tempest-tossed, the harbour of mariners, the Physician of the sick. Be Thou Thyself all things to all people, who knowest each, and his petition and his dwelling and his need.

✠ ✠ ✠ ✠ ✠

From the Liturgy of St. Mark

Visit, O Lord, in Thy pity and mercies, those of Thy people that are sick; those of our brethren that have departed or are about to depart; give to each a prosperous journey in his place...

Heal them that are vexed of unclean spirits, them that are in prisons, or in mines, or in courts of justice, or with sentence given against them or in bitter slavery...Have mercy upon all; free all; ... to every Christian soul that is in trouble give mercy, give refreshment.

A Cry for God's Help

O Lord, forsake me not.
O Lord, do not stand afar off from me
O Lord, stretch out to me a helping hand.
O Lord, support me with the holy fear of You.
O Lord, plant this fear
and the love for You in my heart.
O Lord, teach me to do Your will.
O Lord, give mourning
and humility to my heart.
O Lord, give me unceasing tears, compunction,
and remembrance of death.
O Lord, free me from every temptation of soul
and body.
O Lord, expel from me every unclean thought,
and every shameful and evil imagination.
O Lord, wipe out of me the negligence,
the indolence, the sorrow, the forgetfulness,
the insensitivity, the hardness,
and the captivity of my mind.
O Lord, have mercy on me,
as You know and as You wish,
and forgive all my sins.
And grant that my pitiful soul
may depart from my ailing body
in quietude, in good repentance,
in unhesitating confession,
and in pure and spotless faith. AMEN.   - ST. PAISIOS

✠ ✠ ✠ ✠ ✠

O God, from whom to be turned is to fall,
to whom to be turned is to rise,
and with whom to stand is to abide for ever;
grant us in all our duties Your help,
in all our perplexities Your guidance,
in all our dangers Your protection,
and in all our sorrows Your peace,
through Jesus Christ our Lord, Amen.

–St. Augustine

✠ ✠ ✠ ✠ ✠

Give perfection to beginners, O Father; give intelligence to the little ones; give aid to those who are running their course. Give sorrow to the negligent; give fervour of spirit to the lukewarm. Give to the perfect a good consummation; for the sake of Christ Jesus our Lord. Amen.

- Irenaeus, Second Century

✠ ✠ ✠ ✠ ✠

As the deer pants for streams of water,
so my soul pants for you, O God.
My soul thirsts for God, for the living God.
When can I go and meet with God?
My tears have been my food day and night,
while men say to me all day long,

'Where is your God?'
These things I remember
as I pour out my soul:
how I used to go with the multitude,
leading the procession to the house of God,
with shouts of joy and thanksgiving
among the festive throng.
Why are you downcast, O my soul?
Why so disturbed within me?
Put your hope in God,
for I will yet praise Him,
my Saviour and my God.

—PSALM 42:1-6

✛ ✛ ✛ ✛ ✛

O Lord, Help Me

In silence
    to find peace
    -not just emptiness
In suffering
    to find meaning
    -not just agony
In knowledge
    to find wisdom
    -not just information
In routine
    to find order
    -not just boredom

In order
    to find purpose
    -not just the expected
In daily life
    to find surprises
    -not just conformity
In prayer
    to find YOU
    -not just my own desires
In change
    to find promises
    -not just threats
In opportunities
    to find possibilities
    -not just problems
In sin
    to find forgiveness
    -not just guilt
In problems
    to find hope
    -not just despair
In leadership
    to find direction
    -not just power
In challenges
    to find trust in You
    -not just personal insecurity   AMEN.

✠ ✠ ✠ ✠ ✠

For Disappointment

Lord, I've had such a disappointment today. Something I had hoped for, dreamed of, and yes, even prayed for is just not to be. I'm hurt and I'm angry. Help me to turn loose of this bitterness. Now I see only darkness and despair. Light your lamp within me, O Lord of Light. May I see clearly through this shadow that has fallen across my life. Remind me that just as the darkness of night only hides the day for a few hours, Your light shines on behind the darkness of my difficulties and disappointments. AMEN.

A Vacation Prayer

Dear Lord, how I've waited for this vacation, and now it's finally here. Thank You, Lord, for the opportunity to take a break from my daily routine and to replenish my mind, body, and soul so that I may better serve You. Sometimes my expectations for vacations are unrealistic, and I find myself disappointed when things don't go my way. Help me not to worry about having the "perfect" vacation but to relax and enjoy every moment, whatever it may bring. I am grateful for the joys that await me–whether they be the beauty of your creation, recreation with family or friends, or peace and solitude. Watch over me and protect me as I travel, and bring me safely home again–refreshed and renewed. AMEN.

Prayer of an Expectant Mother

Dear heavenly Father, words cannot express the joy I feel in knowing that soon I will have a child. You have blessed my life in so many ways, but I am especially thankful for this blessing. I am so anxious about the exciting changes taking place within me–physically, emotionally, mentally, and even spiritually. More than ever, Father, I feel Your love filling me and enfolding me. Help me to entrust my worries to Your care, particularly those worries about the health and safety of my baby. Thank You for the precious moments to be shared with my husband, family and friends as we prepare for the birth of this child. I pray that as the child grows within me, I may grow in grace and love.

These things I ask in the name of the Father, the Son and the Holy Spirit. Amen.

For a Busy Day with Children

Father, thank You that I am also a parent. I'm looking forward to this busy day that will be filled with the chatter and laughter of my children. May I catch their enthusiasm and may their interests infect my own spirit so that I, too, may have a childlike eagerness for the events of the day. Give us patience if the day grows long and tempers wear thin. May we end the day with eagerness to spend another day together. AMEN.

When Children Quarrel

O gracious God, Father of us all, I ask You for help and guidance when my children quarrel. Often I wonder how these children, loved as they are, can be so unloving and unlovely. Their teasing, provoking, and fighting hurt me, Lord, and make me lose my temper as well. Grant me patience and understanding. Help me to establish within our home and family an atmosphere of harmony, but help me too, to remember that my children are not adults and that trying their strength is part of growing up. Keep me sane, Lord, calm, and unruffled, ready to quiet, to comfort, and to smile. AMEN.

A Child's First Day at School

Dear God, here is (name), ready for her first day at school. She has been counting the days. She is so thrilled.

Be with her today when she goes into unfamiliar rooms, when she sees new faces (make them kind faces!), when she stands in the lunch line, when she is on the playground. Keep her close to You as she learns and grows and makes friends. Protect her from harm. Watch over her on the way to and from school. And as she becomes part of a larger world, help me to let her go and gain experience that she will need to become a responsible part of Your creation. AMEN.

For a New Mother

My friend's baby has been born! Her first one. How thrilled and touched she sounds! She has finally witnessed a miracle!

Thank You, Lord, for my friend and for this beautiful new life You have entrusted to her and her husband. Today she praises You and thanks You for her precious gift. Bless this new family with Your grace that they might grow ever close to You and to one another. Be with my friend in her joy and in her fatigue; in her nights of fitful sleep; when the baby is crying and she doesn't know why. Help her recall the awe and wonder of this day and to rejoice at the privilege of being an instrument of your ongoing creation. AMEN.

For Those Who
Are Anxious

Live in the Present

God, I spend so much time reliving yesterday or
anticipating tomorrow that I lose sight of the
only time that is really mine...the present.
Remind me that the past...with its successes
and failures...is over.
The future is yet to be, and eagerness and
apprehension will not hasten it...or postpone it.
You give me today, one minute at a time.
That's all I have...all I ever will.
Give me the faith that knows that each moment
contains exactly what is best for me.
Give me the hope that trusts You enough to
forget past sins and future trials.
Give the love that makes each minute of life
an anticipation of eternity with You.   AMEN.

Prayer of Metropolitan Philaret of Moscow:

Lord, I know not what to ask of You. You alone know
what my true needs are. You love me more than I
myself know how to love. Help me to see my real
needs which may be hidden from me. I dare not ask
for either a cross or a consolation. I can only wait
upon You; my heart is open to You. Visit and help me
in Your steadfast love. Strike me and heal me; cast me

down and raise me up. I worship in silence Your holy will. I offer myself to You as a living sacrifice. I put all my trust in You. I have no other desire than to fulfill Your will. Teach me to pray. Pray Yourself in me. AMEN.

Come, My Light

Come, my Light, and illumine my darkness.
Come, my Life, and revive me from death.
Come, my Physician, and heal my wounds.
Come, Flame of divine love, and burn up the thorns of my misdeeds, kindling my heart with the flame of Your love.
Come, my God, sit upon the throne of my heart and reign there.
For You alone are my God and my Lord.

–ST. DIMITRII OF ROSTOV, 17TH CENTURY

For Greater Closeness To God

Closer to You!

My God and my Lord, take me away from my own self, and let me belong completely to You.

My God and my Lord, take away everything that keeps me apart from You.
My God and my Lord, grant me everything that draws me closer to You.   –BY A CHURCH FATHER

Eternal God, Help Us to Know You
A Prayer Based on Augustine
Eternal God,
the light of the minds that know You,
the life of the souls that love You,
the strength of the wills that serve You;
help us so to know You that we may truly love You,
so to love You that we may fully serve You,
whom to serve is perfect freedom.

Prayer for the Beginning of the Church Year

Christ our God,
    Your kingdom is an everlasting one
    and Your lordship is over all.
You have made all things with wisdom
    and have established proper times and seasons
    for our lives.
We give thanks to You in all circumstances and
    for all things, Lord,
bless the beginning of our church year with
    your goodness.
Grant that this liturgical year be for all of us a
    year of grace.
Make us worthy with purity of heart always to
    praise You.
Lord, glory to You!   –MATINS HYMN, 1 SEPTEMBER

When We Don't Know What To Pray For

O Jesus, Word with infinite names,
show me what and how
I should ask from You in my requests.
O Jesus, Son of God, have mercy on me.

St. Nicodemos of Mount Athos

✦ ✦ ✦ ✦ ✦

O Lord, as You command;
O Lord, as You know;
O Lord, as You wish,
so let Your will be done in me.

St. John Chrysostom

✠ ✠ ✠ ✠ ✠

Have mercy on me, O Lord.
Strengthen my soul;
govern the rest of my life towards Your will,
as Your compassion and love for humankind
know best.

St. Basil the Great

A Prayer for Completing Life's Journey in Faith and Love

May I be no one's enemy, and may I be the friend of that which is eternal and abides. May I never quarrel with those nearest me; and if I do, may I be reconciled quickly. May I never devise evil against any one; if any devise evil against me, may I escape uninjured and without the need of hurting them. May I love, seek, and attain that which is good. May I wish for all people's happiness and envy none. May I never rejoice in the ill-fortune of one who has wronged me. When I have done or said that is wrong, may I never wait for the rebuke of others, but always rebuke myself until I make amends. May I win no victory that harms me or my opponent. May I reconcile friends who are angry with one another. May I, to the extent of my power, give all merciful help to my friends and to all those who are in want. May I never fail a friend in danger. When visiting those in grief, may I be able by my gentle and healing words, to soften their pain. May I respect myself. May I always keep tame that which rages within me. May I accustom myself to be gentle, and never be angry with people because of circumstances. May I never discuss who is wicked and what wicked things he has done, but know good men and follow in their footsteps.

–EUSEBIUS: SECOND CENTURY

Love of Life

Adapted from a Passage in "The Brothers of Karamazov"

Lord, may we love all Your creation, all the earth and every grain of sand in it. May we love every leaf, every ray of Your light.

May we love the animals: You have given them the rudiments of thought and joy untroubled. Let us not trouble it; let us not harass them, let us not deprive them of their happiness, let us not work against Your intent.

For we acknowledge unto You that all is like an ocean, all is flowing and blending, and that to withhold any measure of love from anything in Your universe is to withhold that same measure from You.

—Fyodor Dostoevsky

A Prayer For Hope

O Lord our God, under the shadow of Thy wings let us hope. Thou wilt support us, both when little, even to gray hairs. When our strength is of Thee, it is strength; but, when our own, it is feebleness. We return to unto Thee, O Lord, that from their weariness our souls may rise towards Thee, leaning on the things which Thou has created, and passing on to Thyself, who hast wonderfully made them; for with Thee is refreshment and true strength. Amen

– St. Augustine

A Prayer For Light and Guidance

O God our Father, who dost exhort us to pray, and who dost grant what we ask, if only, when we ask, we live a better life; hear me, who am trembling in this darkness, and stretch forth Thy hand unto me; hold forth Thy light before me; recall me from my wanderings; and, Thou being my Guide, may I be restored to myself and to Thee, through Jesus Christ. AMEN.

—ST. AUGUSTINE

Prayers of Forgiveness

O Lord, the house of my soul is narrow;
enlarge it, that you may enter in.
It is ruinous, O repair it!
It displeases your sight; I confess it, I know.
But who shall cleanse it, to whom shall I cry
but to you?
Cleanse me from my secret faults, O Lord,
and spare your servant from strange sins.

—ST. AUGUSTINE

✛ ✛ ✛ ✛ ✛

O Lord,
I praise, bless, venerate, glorify,
and thank Your goodness
for all, through all, and in all;
for You have delivered my soul from death,
my eyes from tears
and my feet from slipping.
I have sinned against heaven
and before You.
Have mercy on me, O Lord,
and do not destroy me
together with my sins.
Test me, O God,
and examine my paths;
see if there is a way of transgression in me,
and turn me away from it;
and lead me into the eternal way, O God,
You who have said:
I am the way and the truth and the life,
for You are blessed unto the ages. Amen.

–St. Macarius

A Prayer for the Faithful Stewardship of Life

O Lord God Almighty, who has built Thy Church upon the foundation of the Apostles, under Christ the head cornerstone, and to this end didst endow Thy holy apostle St. Barnabas with the singular gift of the Holy Ghost; leave me not destitute, I humbly beseech Thee, of Thy manifold gifts and talents, nor yet of grace to make a right use of them always without any sordid self-ends, to Thy honour and glory; that, making a due improvement of all those gifts Thou graciously entrustest me with, I may be able to give a good account of my stewardship when the great Judge shall appear, the Lord Jesus Christ, who reigneth with Thee and the Eternal Spirit, one God, blessed forever. AMEN.

- BARNABAS, SECOND CENTURY

Other Publications by Light & Life Publishing Company

REQUEST A FREE CATALOG

Light and Life Publishing Company   P.O. Box 26421   Minneapolis, Minnesota 55426-0421
Visit our website: http://www.light-n-life.com   E-Mail: info@light-n-life.com   Phone: 1-(952)-925-3888

This is one of many books published by:

www .light-n-life.com
Browse our catalog on-
line and place your order
24 hours a day!
Be sure to bookmark our
website and add it to
your "favorite places!"

Serving you for 35 years.
1966-2001

World's Largest Orthodox Supplier

Books - Icons - Crosses - CDs - etc.
1-(952)-925-3888 Mon.-Fri. 9:00a.m.- 5:00p.m. CST

Cut here and mail coupon to Light & Life to receive your free catalog.